NAFTA and Sovereignty

Significant Issues Series

SIGNIFICANT ISSUES SERIES papers are written for and published by the Center for Strategic and International Studies.

Director of Studies: Erik R. Peterson

Director of Publications: James R. Dunton

Managing Editor: Roberta L. Howard

Editorial Assistant: Kathleen M. McTigue

The Center for Strategic and International Studies (CSIS), established in 1962, is a private, tax-exempt institution focusing on international public policy issues. Its research is nonpartisan and nonproprietary.

CSIS is dedicated to policy analysis and impact. It seeks to inform and shape selected policy decisions in government and the private sector to meet the increasingly complex and difficult global challenges that leaders will confront in the next century. It achieves this mission in three ways: by generating strategic analysis that is anticipatory and interdisciplinary; by convening policymakers and other influential parties to assess key issues; and by building structures for policy action.

CSIS does not take specific public policy positions. Accordingly, all views, positions, and conclusions expressed in this publication should be understood to be solely those of the authors.

❖   ❖   ❖

The Center for Strategic and International Studies
1800 K Street, N.W.
Washington, D.C.   20006
Telephone: (202) 887-0200
Fax: (202) 775-3199
E-mail: info@csis.org
Web site: http://www.csis.org/

NAFTA and Sovereignty
Trade-offs for Canada, Mexico, and the United States

Edited by *Joyce Hoebing*
Sidney Weintraub, and
M. Delal Baer

THE CENTER FOR STRATEGIC & INTERNATIONAL STUDIES
Washington, D.C.

Significant Issues Series, Volume XVIII, Number 4
© 1996 by The Center for Strategic and International Studies
Washington, D.C. 20006
Printed on recycled paper in the United States of America

99 98 97 96   5 4 3 2 1

ISSN 0736-7136
ISBN 0-89206-322-X

Library of Congress Cataloging-in-Publication Data

NAFTA and sovereignty : trade-offs for Canada, Mexico, and the
  United States / editors, Joyce Hoebing, Sidney Weintraub, M. Delal Baer.
     p. cm. — (Significant issues series, ISSN 0736-7136 ; v. 18, no. 4)
  ISBN 0-89206-322-X
    1. Free trade—North America. 2. North America—
Economic integration. 3. Canada. Treaties, etc. 1992 Oct. 7.
I. Hoebing, Joyce, 1960– . II. Weintraub, Sidney, 1922– .
III. Baer, M. Delal, 1953– . IV. Series
HF176.N32 1996
382'.917--dc20   96-30473
                                               CIP

Contents

UNITED STATES

About the Contributors

M. Delal Baer is director of the Mexico Project and senior fellow at the Center for Strategic and International Studies. She co-chairs the Advanced Area Seminar on Mexico at the U.S. State Department's Foreign Service Institute and has taught as an adjunct faculty member at the University of Maryland and Georgetown and George Mason Universities. She is the author of "The New Order and Disorder in U.S.-Mexican Relations," in *A New North America: Cooperation and Free Trade*, edited by Charles F. Doran and Alvin Paul Drischler (Praeger, 1996). She received her B.A. in history from George Washington University and her Ph.D. in political science from the University of Michigan.

Charles F. Doran is the Andrew W. Mellon Professor of International Relations and director of the Center of Canadian Studies at the Paul H. Nitze School of Advanced International Studies (SAIS), Johns Hopkins University. He has taught at Rice University and the University of Toronto and is the author of more than 50 scholarly articles and books on international politics and political economy.

Jonathan Heath is an economist specializing in matters relating to the Mexican economy. An independent consultant, he has worked with Mexico's Ministry of Budget and Planning, the Wharton Econometric Forecasting Associates, and MACRO Asesoria Economica. He has written prolifically on the Mexican economic outlook and related topics, including *The Devaluation of the Mexican Peso in 1994* (Washington, D.C.: Center for Strategic and International Studies, 1995) *and The Impact of Mexico's Trade Liberalization* (Baltimore, Md.: Johns Hopkins University Press, forthcoming).

Joyce Hoebing is assistant director of the Americas Program at the Center for Strategic and International Studies. She is the editor of the *Western Hemisphere Election Study Series*, the *Policy Papers on the Americas* series, and *Hemisphere 2000*. She coordinates the Caribbean Leadership Project and was the editor of *Leadership in the Caribbean: Working Papers* (Washington, D.C.: Center for Strategic and International Studies, 1996). She received an M.B.A. in finance and international business from the University of Chicago.

Federico Reyes Heroles, a Mexican writer and political commentator, is director of the magazine *Este Pais* and a regular contributor to the political editorial sections of the Mexican newspapers *Reforma* and *El Norte*. He is currently a visiting lecturer at the University of Chicago. Reyes Heroles received his bachelor's degree in philosophy from the Autonomous National University of Mexico.

Murray G. Smith is an international economic consultant based in Geneva, Switzerland. Previously, he was director of the Centre for Trade Policy and Law, Carleton University and the University of Ottawa, and before that director of the International Economics Program of the Institute for Research on Public Policy, Canada. He is the author of many articles and books on Canada-U.S. economic relations, the Canada-U.S. Free Trade Agreement, NAFTA, the Uruguay Round of trade negotiations, and the implications of globalization for economic policy.

Denis Stairs is professor of political science at Dalhousie University in Halifax, Nova Scotia. A former president of the Canadian Political Science Association, he was vice president (academic and research) at Dalhousie from 1988 to 1993. He is the author of *The Diplomacy of Constraint: Canada, the Korean War, and the United States* (Toronto: University of Toronto Press, 1974) and other works on Canadian foreign and defense policy, Canadian-American relations, and related subjects.

Sidney Weintraub, an economist, holds the William E. Simon Chair in Political Economy at the Center for Strategic and International Studies. He is also Dean Rusk Professor of International Affairs at the Lyndon B. Johnson School of Public Affairs, University of Texas at Austin. He is the sole author or editor of more than 15 books and 135 articles, including *A Marriage of Convenience: Relations between Mexico and the United States* (Oxford University Press, 1990), *NAFTA—What Comes Next?* (Praeger for the

Center for Strategic and International Studies, 1994), and *NAFTA at Three: A Progress Report* (Center for Strategic and International Studies, forthcoming). He received his Ph.D. in economics from American University and his M.A. in economics from Yale University.

Preface

Today's global climate and the increasingly blurred distinction between domestic and international policy invite a redefinition of sovereignty both conceptually and in practice. Multilateral trade agreements in particular are viewed by many as significant symbols of loss of sovereignty. From the manufacturing worker who is anxious about lower-wage countries "stealing" his job to the economically developing country that fears a diminution of its own capacity for political and economic decision-making because of enhanced ties to a larger economy, sovereignty is an issue that brings emotions to the fore. Sovereignty declines, however, are not occurring solely because of more integrated trade; sovereignty is being influenced by a host of factors, including global communication, capital flows, and the Internet.

The process of economic integration among the United States, Canada, and Mexico implies a larger degree of political cooperation than has existed heretofore. Fear of the associated diminution of sovereignty has at times resonated deeply in each of the North American countries: it was invoked in Mexico and the United States in the debate over the North American Free Trade Agreement (NAFTA), and in Canada during the Canada-U.S. Free Trade Agreement (CUFTA) negotiations. Both Ross Perot in 1992 and Pat Buchanan in 1996 tried to use loss of sovereignty due to NAFTA as a rallying call in their respective populist campaigns for the U.S. presidency. In Mexico, which historically has felt the need to guard its sovereignty against incursions—economic, political, and territorial—by the United States, the issue of sovereignty was surprisingly minimized in the free trade debate, but had been used repeatedly in the past to garner support for protectionism. And in Canada, which has its own internal sovereignty concerns, the increasingly close economic relationship with the United States has raised concerns over cultural sovereignty.

Sovereignty, the ability to both defend a nation's territory from outside aggressors and make policy decisions free from outside influence, is viewed today very differently than it was when the term originated. The existence of multilateral organizations such as the United Nations and the North Atlantic Treaty Organization, increased access to information through revolutions in the telecommunications field, and the forging of multilateral agreements on issues such as trade-dispute resolutions, all interact to alter the context in which sovereignty is viewed.

Increased economic integration in North America implies the ceding of some autonomy in decision-making by each of the three countries. Because of its greater power to make and act on unilateral decisions, the United States arguably gives up more when it agrees to trade-dispute resolution mechanisms than do its two smaller neighbors. On the other hand, Canada is wary of the potential for the United States to influence its ability to retain a separate culture, and both Canada and Mexico are concerned about their ability to formulate their own, distinct foreign policies. These worries, however, may be exaggerated. It is not clear that any of the countries is in fact giving up its core decision-making ability, especially because NAFTA is a free trade agreement rather than a customs union, which would require coordinated commercial policy. Further, when entering into a free trade agreement, a country presumably receives benefits that outweigh the costs of relinquishing some sovereignty.

Still, the issues surrounding sovereignty have important policy implications for the United States. Nontraditional issues, including not just sovereignty but labor standards, the environment, and a host of other concerns, have become integral parts of debates over trade agreements. Sensitivities both within and outside the United States must be better understood, and negotiations for expanding free trade throughout the hemisphere must incorporate strategies to minimize friction over these issues.

This publication was conceived by CSIS to explore Canadian, Mexican, and U.S. conceptions of sovereignty and national hang-ups concerning the issue, as well as the ensuing implications for the countries and their trilateral relationship. An economist and a political scientist from each country were asked to explore these issues. The results indicate that each country has indeed given up some sovereignty. Yet, although increased trade integration may have contributed to this fact, it is by no means a simple causal relationship.

On the Canadian side, Denis Stairs argues that although sovereignty in Canada has decreased in the traditional sense given Canada's trade dependence on the United States, the approval of CUFTA in 1988 and the operation since mark the decline of the public's concern over the issue. Murray G. Smith of Canada examines the sovereignty issues that were raised in the debate over CUFTA and NAFTA, such as loss of political autonomy and "deindustrialization" of the Canadian economy—and demonstrates that these concerns were not realized.

Jonathan Heath writes that in Mexico sovereignty is an issue that is invoked primarily when the country's political and economic elite attempt to consolidate their power. He argues that sovereignty for the country as a whole (i.e., increasing the economic and political decision-making capability of the nation's majority) has neither improved nor declined. Federico Reyes Heroles approaches Mexico's concerns over sovereignty by defining sovereignty in terms of four different dimensions—doctrinal, discourse, factual, and subjective. His analysis implies that the Mexican people are much less threatened by the power to the north than might be believed by official discourse.

Charles F. Doran examines the history of sovereignty in an attempt to identify the theoretical underpinnings of the concept and thereby increase understanding of U.S. concerns with the issues surrounding loss of sovereignty. Finally, Sidney Weintraub argues that while some sovereignty is given up in exchange for the benefits of free trade (a long-existing trend of give and take), in fact the United States retains the most fundamental aspect of sovereignty—the ability to determine its own key national policies.

The editors would like to thank the Andrew W. Mellon Foundation, whose support made this study possible.

1

The Canadian Dilemma in North America

Denis Stairs

Our anxiety about national survival is attributable to fear of our own failure of will.[1]

John W. Holmes—that most thoughtful of Canadian scholar-diplomats—first made the above observation during a series of seminars on Canadian nationalism in the winter of 1964–1965. In Ontario especially, and among intellectuals in particular, the fear to which he referred was then deeply felt. It can be argued now that it has largely disappeared. It could certainly recur. And self-indulgent Americans in high congressional places could easily *make* it recur. But unless and until it does, its departure leaves some obvious questions. Why does Canadian nationalism (in its explicit form, at least) appear to have declined? How far has it gone? Has it taken with it any of the traditional Canadian attachments to sovereignty? What concerns—active or latent—still remain? Are they likely to affect the Canada-U.S. relationship? In short, should Americans care?

After a brief reminder of some of the more obvious features of the Canadian nation-building experience, this chapter will begin by focusing on the character of such nationalist ruminations as were evident in Canada in the postwar period, particularly in the 1960s and 1970s. It will then consider the reasons for the weakening of nationalist preoccupations among dominant Canadian elites in the 1980s. These matters are not readily susceptible to hard proof, and the analysis therefore will be more speculative than definitive. The persuasive power of the circumstantial evidence may nonetheless seem difficult to deny.

The exploration will conclude with an evaluation of the character and significance of the sorts of issues that remain, together with an assessment of their implications for policymakers

in Canada, and of the degree to which they may or may not intrude on the political agenda of the United States. Any effect on
the U.S. political agenda, as it turns out, may depend more on
U.S. behavior than on Canadian. From the vantage point of
Canada-U.S. relations, Canadian nationalism is for the most
part a sleeping dog. If the dog wakes up, the stimulus for its
arousal is more likely to originate south of the Canada-U.S. border than north of it. [2] In the meantime, the Canadian dilemma itself can best be understood as an early (but now well-advanced)
manifestation of a rapidly globalizing phenomenon.

Imagining the Canadian Community

In Benedict Anderson's arresting phrase, nations are "imagined
communities,"[3] and nationalism itself has been described by
Isaiah Berlin as "an inflamed condition of national conscious-
ness."[4] Such imaginings, inflamedly conscious or otherwise, are
often the product of contrivance—both political and intellectual—and there may be a sense in which the nationalism of
Canadians has been more contrived than most. They have had to
work at it. In defining themselves, they have tried to draw on
their political practices and constitutional traditions as the most
promising—and the least menacing to liberal democratic ide-
als—of the potential grounds on which to assert a distinctive
identity. Edmund Burke would have approved. But Canadians
cannot set themselves apart from others (as the protégés of the
French Enlightenment were wont to do two centuries ago and as
Americans are still wont to do now) by claiming original author-
ship and custody of a corpus of political principles presumed to
be rightly universal. Nor, in their pursuit of self-definition, can
they have recourse to distinguishing histories and mythologies
of the volk—whether real, invented, or a mixture of the two—
after the pattern of Germans, Slavs, and other Europeans of similar mind, past and present.

For Canadians, the difficulty of the nation-building enterprise—of the task, that is, of constructing an imagined community within which they can feel as psychologically fulfilled as
they are practically served—is complicated by the diversity of
their own ethnic origins, a diversity that is steadily increasing.
Nation-building is rendered more intricate still by the long-
standing bifurcation of their community into French- and English-speaking components. And it is plagued as well by the
absence in their history of dramatic events that could be genera-

tive of dramatic myths. They had no revolution, no civil war, no cataclysm (save the winters with which they annually cope) that they could call uniquely their own.[5]

In such a context, they have been compelled to regard the humdrum habits of pragmatic politics as their defining virtue, and their symbols (as they often ruefully observe to themselves) reflect their practical disposition. The industrious beaver, not the soaring eagle, is their national mark in the animal world (and the beaver, in some parts of their country, is fast becoming an unacceptably destructive pest!). The leitmotiv of their constitutional litany is peace, order, and good government. Unlike life, liberty, and the pursuit of happiness, it does little to encourage competitive individuals to acquire property and to achieve excellence in an environment in which opportunities abound. But it does much to remind a skeptical citizenry of the importance of restraint, and the value of stability in a world in which hazards proliferate.

Again, the symbolic custodian of justice in Canada is not the lonely cowboy hero, armed with six-gun, courage, and a clear sense of right and wrong, but a polished para-soldier, an agent of the state—the red-coated officer-on-horseback of the Royal Canadian Mounted Police (RCMP). It is Americans, moreover, not Canadians, who put him in their musicals—although even they, sensing that the symbol is regarded in Canada with more analytical detachment than emotional fervor, do so only with tongue in cheek. Canadians, meanwhile, have been prepared to license the Mountie's image to the Walt Disney Company for purposes of commercial exploitation. The uniform may be uniquely Canadian, and the use of it on ceremonial occasions may well be an honest reflection of a culturally transmitted respect for authority and a continuing attachment to order; but the image is not sacrosanct, and if it can be usefully deployed in the service of paying the bills, so be it.[6]

Still again, the most popular analysis of Canadian literature, written by one of the most accomplished of Canadian authors, argues that the central figures in Canadian fiction are not heroes, but victims, and that the task assigned to them is not victory, but survival.[7] By extension to the real world, adversities (sometimes including adversities emanating from the Great Republic) can rarely be beaten down or beaten back. A wise policy therefore reflects a more modest aspiration. It seeks to moderate, to live with, to accommodate—in short, to survive by limiting the damage.

All this may serve well enough to sustain a sensible political praxis, but it offers mediocre nourishment for communal romantics.[8] It also makes it harder to think of the whole as greater than the sum of its parts and, hence, to regard the national collective as a source of personal inspiration. The task of cultivating a Canadian national imagination may thus have much in common with the challenge confronting nation builders in the postcolonial states of the contemporary developing world, many of which are geographical expressions whose political boundaries bear little relation to the local distribution of ethnic or tribal loyalties. A Canadian community may have correspondingly less in common with the experience of the culturally homogeneous countries of Western Europe or with that of the United States, whose identity was forged more than 200 years ago in a political philosophy sanctified by revolution and preserved later by civil war.

Having said that, it must be said as well that the attempt to imagine a community in Canada has a much longer history than in the freshly emergent countries of the contemporary postcolonial world, and it has come as much from the bottom up as from the top down. In English-Canada, at least, the imagining itself was suffused throughout the course of its prolonged beginning with a loyalty to monarchy and empire and with a not unrelated distrust of revolutionary optimism. These dispositions clearly differentiated Canada's politics from those of the United States, and it can be argued that they still profoundly influence its political culture, albeit in greatly modified form. Many of the differences in Canadian and U.S. public policies have their origins in this underlying reality, and so do many of the diplomatic tiffs and clashes that sporadically disturb the otherwise amiable tenor of the Canada-U.S. relationship.

Recent Imaginings Recently Applied: The 1960s and 1970s

In recent decades, Canadian preoccupations with imagining a national identity were expressed most explicitly during the political debates of the 1960s and 1970s. For Americans who were attentive to these debates at the time (perhaps it is fortunate there were not very many), the arguments at issue were often a source of puzzlement and sometimes a cause of irritation. They will be familiar even now to cognoscenti.[9] But a brief reminder of the most important of the issues debated may none-

theless be useful if only because they had practical policy implications and because a review of them will lend perspective to
current realities. Their relevance in the present context is rendered especially acute because in every case they came to a head
as a result of the fear of U.S. dominance, a fear that generated
precisely the anxiety to which John Holmes, in the winter of
1964–1965, found it appropriate to refer.

Foreign Policy

Of the various concerns at issue, the one that related most immediately and directly to the conduct of Canada-U.S. relations had
to do with the question of Canada's capacity to pursue international political-security policies that were in some reasonable
measure independent of those of the United States. *Dependence*
and *independence* are concepts whose pertinence to the understanding of particular cases rests only partly on what the evidence may demonstrate. Their pertinence depends also on the
standards and expectations that the observer brings to bear.
Debates on the subject, therefore, tend to be rooted in ambiguous combinations of fact, perception, and political predisposi-
tion—a circumstance that makes them intellectually difficult to
resolve and encourages the debaters themselves to prolong the
argument. In Canada's case, the first significant traces of angst
on foreign policy could be detected in the political discourse of
the social democratic left. This was represented in the early years
of the postwar period by the Cooperative Commonwealth Federation, which changed its name to its current designation, the
New Democratic Party, at the beginning of the 1960s.

Social democracy as a political orientation has received only
the faintest of expressions in the United States, but in Canada it
has strong roots as a kind of third force. In foreign affairs, its traditions have been consistently internationalist. Guided by an
egalitarian political philosophy grounded in an optimistic view
of human nature and a corresponding distrust of the "power
politics" approach to the conduct of international relations, its
supporters displayed even in the 1950s a certain uneasiness over
the uncompromisingly rough-and-tumble prosecution of the
cold war by the United States and its allies (Liberal and Conservative governments in Ottawa included). They were inclined to
think that strategies of accommodation would lead more reliably
to pacific outcomes. Because there was little prospect of modify-
ing the behavior of the United States (or, for that matter, the

countries of Western Europe) from within, there were sugges-
tions that Canada might make a more constructive contribution
to the international order by branching out on its own.

In the Canadian foreign policy literature (such as it was at
the time), this general disposition came most elaborately to the
fore in 1960 in a small book written by the Canadian Broadcasting Corporation's radio correspondent in Washington, James M.
Minifie. Canada, he thought, was "caught in a too-close alliance
which gives it the appearance of subordination to the United
States." This was unacceptable, not least because "in climbing to
the paramountcy, the United States [had] acquired some of the
attributes, and more of the reputation, of military, political and
economic imperialism." The result was that anti-Americanism
was "everywhere" and in Canada took the form of "a chip-on-
the-shoulder inferiority complex based on the suspicion that
Canadian independence, so patiently won from Britain, [was]
being swiftly eroded by U.S. military, economic and cultural
domination." There was a solution, however, and "Canadian
independence [could] be restored." It required only an "understanding of the problem by Canadians . . ., an exposition of the
problem and the proposed remedy to the Americans, and then a
resolute application of the remedy in a vivid and memorable act,
as readily recognizable as the Declaration of Independence."
That act would be a "Declaration of Neutralism," entailing Canada's withdrawal from NATO, NORAD, and the Permanent
Joint Board on Defence. This would make possible the deploy-
ment of Canadian diplomatic assets from a neutral, not a satellite, posture. The effect, Minifie argued, would be to render
Canada more credible in the world at large and, hence, more
effective as an actor in the pursuit of international peace.[10]

There was a rejoinder by political scientist and former diplo-
mat Peyton V. Lyon, who argued that it was a grave mistake to
assume that adopting a policy of neutralism would increase
Canada's diplomatic influence. In the first place, Canada was
badly positioned to offer a convincing performance in a neutral
role. Second, Canada's reputation as a reliable ally was among
the most important of its diplomatic assets. A significant source
of diplomatic credit in Washington and European capitals alike,
Canada's reputation gave its representatives a seat at the table
and, hence, an opportunity to affect the development of allied
policy. This was evident not only to Canada's friends but also to
third parties. It therefore lent credibility to Canadian representations in a variety of forums abroad. It also strengthened the

ability of Canadian diplomats to act as channels through which sensitive arguments might be constructively conveyed to the occupants of higher office in the capitals of the greater powers. And for all this, the modest prerequisite was the payment of a modest fee: participation in the North Atlantic Alliance and in cooperative arrangements with the United States for the defense of North America.[11]

Minifie offered a further elaboration of his case in a sequel published in 1964,[12] but the focus on foreign policy as the measure of Canada's independence did not really acquire a significant visibility, even among members of the interested public, until 1968. That was the year in which Stephen Clarkson, a young professor with the Department of Political Economy at the University of Toronto, edited a series of essays under the title *An Independent Foreign Policy for Canada?*[13] The essays originated as presentations to a series of seminars conducted during the 1966–1967 academic year. The contributors did not all address the same topic nor did they necessarily agree on substance; but the predominant theme, as identified and elaborated by the editor, was a concern with the preference in Ottawa (and in Washington) for conducting the Canada-U.S. relationship in accordance with the principles of "quiet diplomacy."

The focus on diplomatic practice was stimulated in part by a study that had been conceived at a summit meeting of President Lyndon B. Johnson and Prime Minister Lester B. Pearson in January 1964. The study was undertaken by a two-person working group established in the following month and composed of the former Canadian ambassador to the United States, A.D.P. Heeney, and the former U.S. ambassador to Canada, Livingston T. Merchant. Their task was to examine "the desirability and practicability of developing acceptable principles which would make it easier to avoid divergences in economic and other policies of interest" to the two countries. Their report duly appeared in June 1965, and on the basis largely of a series of case-studies in Canada-U.S. relations, it offered a number of "guiding principles." Among these was the suggestion, in recognition of the "heavy responsibilities borne by the United States, generally as the leader of the free world, and specifically under its network of mutual defense treaties around the globe," that it was "important and reasonable that Canadian authorities should have careful regard for the U.S. government's position in this world context and, in the absence of special Canadian interests or obligations, avoid so far as possible, public disagreement especially on critical issues." This did not mean "that the Canadian Government should automatically and uniformly concur in foreign policy decisions taken by the United States," but it was "in the abiding interest of both countries that, wherever possible, divergent views between the two governments should be expressed and if possible resolved in private, through diplomatic channels."[14]

There was nothing unusual about the premise of this argument, which has a long history in the how-to-do-it literature of diplomatic practice as well as in manuals on negotiating processes more generally. But it was here being advanced in a context that gave encouragement to suspicion. Just two years before, the minority government of John G. Diefenbaker had been brought down for reasons not unrelated to Canada-U.S. defense cooperation. Since then, the involvement of the United States in the Vietnam War had escalated dramatically. Although Canada was not a combatant in the contest, its enthusiastic participation in continental defense production-sharing arrangements made it possible for Canadian critics of the war to complain that Ottawa was guilty of international misbehavior not only by association with the principal perpetrator but also as a profit-seeking economic accessory to U.S. military policy.

By 1966 and 1967, when the Clarkson seminars were in full swing, the Vietnam controversy had heated up and had generated in some quarters an intensifying concern that Canadian policymakers were being co-opted by their U.S. counterparts.[15] According to this view, a loss of independence had ensued that applied not only to the contest in Vietnam but also to Canada's role in the political-security affairs of the world at large. It applied as well to Ottawa's capacity (and even to its will) to give vigorous protection to Canadian interests in bilateral negotiations with Washington. The prevalence of the practices of quiet diplomacy—the practices that the Heeney-Merchant report had so explicitly advocated—were thus taken to be both the indicator and the instrument of the co-optive process. By isolating themselves from public scrutiny, Canadian authorities in the foreign policy field were not merely weakening the mechanisms by which they were held accountable to their constituents; they were depriving themselves of precisely the stimulus that would strengthen their resolve in dealing with the U.S. government and that would prevent them from falling too easily into a comfortable acceptance of U.S. positions. The solution was to open up the policy process, to change the quiescent ideology of the professional foreign service, and to engage the political leadership in the pursuit of a more dynamic and independent approach.[16]

This analysis won little favor with the authorities, professional or political, in Ottawa.[17] Because Canadian diplomatic behavior did not change as a result of it, the quiet diplomacy debate had little substantive impact on Canada-U.S. relations.[18] No domestic U.S. interest was affected. No U.S. public servant was inconvenienced.[19] Hence no U.S. citizen, other than the occasional academic observer, had cause to think the issue was other than the manifestation of an internal Canadian eccentricity. But it was a signal nonetheless of a discontent that was soon to acquire a more intrusive significance. This was because it took an economic turn.

Economic Policy

Economic nationalism in Canada was not a new phenomenon in the 1960s. The nationalist impulse, driven largely by vested economic interests but finding its political ammunition in a continuing public preoccupation with the threat of U.S. dominance, could be detected in debates on the Canada-U.S. trading relationship even before Confederation in the middle of the nineteenth century.[20] The same issue subsequently helped to defeat a Liberal government in 1911. It developed a new head of steam in the 1960s, when the immediate cause of concern had less to do with trade and more to do with direct investment.

To understand this phenomenon, it is necessary to think in terms of premises that predate the ones that are associated with the process we have recently come to describe as economic globalization. Three decades ago it was still widely assumed that governments (in the developed world, at least) had a significant capacity to influence the course of international economic exchange and to modify its impact on respective national economies. Some might think it a poor economic policy to attempt this, but most governments tried it anyway, and certainly few of them thought it technically impossible. Leaving the economy to the "invisible hand" was an option, not an inescapable necessity.

For some of the intellectuals in Canada who had been alerted first to what they perceived as a loss of independence in foreign policy, a decision to focus instead on the issue of U.S. penetration of the Canadian economy (largely by way of direct investment and, more particularly, through the takeover of

Canadian business enterprises) represented a shift to a significantly different view of cause-and-effect relationships.

The complaint about quiet diplomacy had led very easily to a critique of its practitioners (the diplomats themselves) and to remedies for changing their behavior. But what if this behavior was rooted not in the personal and professional inclinations of members of the foreign service and their political masters, nor even in the representations of the neighboring superpower, but in the forces kicked up by the domestic political environment to which the decision-makers in Ottawa were responsible and by which they were most heavily influenced? *Social* democrats would presumably be led to this conclusion very quickly. It would accord, after all, with their tendency to assume that the exercise of political power, unless countervailed by carefully engineered egalitarian processes, will give the most faithful service to the interests of those who occupy the commanding heights of the economy. But *liberal* democrats, noticing a powerful alien presence in the domestic constituency—a presence capable of distorting the normal play of indigenous pluralistic forces—could easily come to a very similar view of the problem if not to quite the same assessment of the solution.

Simply conceived, this view of the problem was that the Canadian economy was in large measure owned and, hence, controlled by foreign interests, most of them located or headquartered in the United States. Canada's economic structure was thus dominated by the branch plants of U.S.-based multinational corporations. This, in turn, had the effect of generating powerful political forces within Canada that policymakers in Ottawa (and in the provinces) could ill afford to ignore. The consequences were manifested, it was argued, in both the private and public sectors, and many of the consequences were contrary to the Canadian interest.

Prominent among the concerns in relation to the private sector was the suspicion that the branch-plant structure was undermining the growth and efficiency of the Canadian economy as a whole. It was argued inter alia that Canadian branch plants of U.S. firms were discouraged by their owners from competing with their parent enterprises for access to export markets; that multinational enterprises tended to concentrate their research and development (R&D) operations in their head offices and home countries, with the result that opportunities to create an indigenous R&D capacity in Canada were being lost; that senior management appointments were similarly dominated by citizens of the countries of origin of the multinationals, and that Canadians, under branch-plant conditions, had a diminished capacity to acquire and propagate their own managerial and entrepreneurial skills at the highest levels; that in times of recession multinationals were inclined to contract their branch-plant operations first, thereby exporting to the branch-plant host a disproportionate share of their excess capacity and disemployment; and, finally, that the branch-plant system had the effect more generally of creating an industrial and manufacturing structure that was geared to the service of a relatively small domestic market and, hence, sacrificed the efficiency and competitiveness associated with a fuller exploitation of economies of scale.

In addition, corporate enterprises operating on a multinational level were in a position, through internal transfer pricing practices, to attribute their profits to the jurisdiction in which they had the greatest tax advantage. In concrete terms, if Canadian corporate taxes were higher than U.S. corporate taxes, accountants in the pay of the multinationals would ensure that corporate profits showed up in U.S. ledgers rather than Canadian. The effect was to deprive Canadian public authorities of revenues appropriate to the real earnings in Canada of the firms in question.

Finally, the ownership of so much of the Canadian economic structure by U.S. enterprises had the effect of subjecting economic activities within Canada to the provisions of U.S. trading-with-the-enemy legislation. This was perceived to be a violation not only of Canada's autonomy but also of its sovereignty, and it had political and economic implications both at home and abroad.[21]

Taken only this far, the implication of the argument was that the problem could be resolved simply be ensuring that enterprises in Canada were predominantly Canadian-owned. Released from the strictures of foreign ownership and a branch-plant structure, Canadian firms would respond naturally to market conditions in a way that would much better serve the Canadian interest. In essence, it was a matter of replacing U.S. ownership with Canadian ownership or, at least, of ensuring that U.S. ownership was kept within reasonable balance. This might require government regulation. It might also call for government manipulation of economic incentives. But once it was ensured that the players would be predominantly Canadian nationals, there would be no further need to disturb the game.

For the social democratic left, however, the analysis had to be taken one step further. If the political purpose was egalitarian and, more specifically, if it was to generate public policies that had the effect of promoting a more equal distribution of wealth, securing the command of the economy in the hands of Canadian (as opposed to American) capitalists would do little to advance the cause. Conceivably, it could help in the long run to enlarge the economic pie. Conceivably, too, it could increase the revenues accruing to Canadian governments and, hence, improve on their capacity to deliver public services. But its most significant impact would be to enhance the privilege of the already privileged. A social democratic society required that the control of the economy, or at least of its commanding heights, be in public, not private, hands. Because it was currently in private hands that were as much foreign as domestic, the transition to social justice would require an economic nationalism that entailed a much more extensive governmental invasion of the marketplace than the one advocated by liberal moderates. The opposition to such an enterprise would come not merely from the agents of capitalism at home but also from the agents of capitalism abroad, particularly in the United States.

The social democratic version of the economic nationalist case was not politically successful (although not for want of effort on the part of its advocates).[22] Canadians have been prepared, in their pragmatic way, to pick bits and pieces of public policy off the social democratic shelf but not to buy the doctrine whole. Serious attempts were made, however, to act on the more moderate liberal version: some failed to get off the ground, and others crashed after a brief flight. Only a few managed to stay in the air for a long period of time. The political weather that has accounted for these mixed outcomes has come partly (although not entirely) from outside the country, notably from the United States. In a moment it will be instructive briefly to consider the significance of this experience.

Cultural Policy

Nationalism in Canada has had other strains in addition to those focused on foreign policy and the economy. Among the most important of these strains has been culture. It may even be said that the cultural field is the one that has created the most perplexing of the practical and philosophical problems confronting the makers of Canadian public policy.

The persistence of the cultural issue on the Canadian agenda derives partly, and most obviously, from an overwhelming U.S. presence in almost every field of public communication. This phenomenon is seemingly unstoppable and unending, and it shows up again and again with the development of each new communications technology. Canadian newsstands are dominated by U.S. magazines. Canadian theaters are dominated by U.S. films (and film distributors). Canadian television is dominated by U.S. channels, and Canadian channels by U.S. programming. Canadian commercial book publishing is largely controlled by U.S. firms. The deafening popular music through which Canadian youths seek to express their adolescent angst is largely American in style when it is not American in origin. So are the celebrities that excite the gossipy imaginations of Canadians young and old alike. Even the paradigms that typically prevail in the academic departments of Canadian universities—those in the humanities and social sciences not least—reflect the voluminous power of U.S. scholarship, U.S. journals, and U.S. (or U.S.-trained) professors. No fantasy, no fad, no consumer's appetite that surfaces in the United States fails to surface in Canada, although it may arrive more slowly and (sometimes) more moderately. Even Canada's sources of international news are largely American, and their power seemingly makes it easier for students in Canadian schools to identify the president of the United States than name the prime minister of the country they call their own.

The attempt to cope with these phenomena raises a prior question: should they be coped with at all? Do they really represent problems, and, if so, are they the sorts of problems that governments ought to address?

Understandably, the U.S. response to these questions has usually been negative, although U.S. governments have been willing in many cases to resign themselves, albeit in dubious and puzzled spirit, to a pragmatic acceptance of Canadian sensibilities. In the first place, it has apparently seemed to them that this is a field in which the state should mind its own business. Keen advocates of the liberal tradition may quarrel over the extent to which the state ought, or ought not, to intrude on the free workings of the market economy. But surely no supporter of the liberal conception of the good society can believe (conventional issues of morality-based censorship aside) that governments should impede the free flow of written or electronic communications. The competitive play of ideas is at the heart of a free community and of the democratic process. The citizens of a liberal state should surely be free to read, hear, and watch whatever they wish without being manipulated by government authorities who presume to know better than they do what is good for them. The consumers of culture, in this view, should be allowed to vote with their feet.

In the second place, Americans have never been entirely persuaded that the issue is in fact a cultural one. The recipients of Hollywood Oscar awards routinely give thanks in their acceptance speeches for the joy that comes from working in what they describe as an industry, and those who negotiate for the U.S. government abroad have usually taken a similar view of the cinematic occupation. For them, culture is high-brow. All the rest is commerce. It follows that those who proclaim themselves to be the diplomatic defenders of Canada's cultural survival are concealing their real purpose, which is nothing more noble than protecting a mildly exotic array of indigenous economic enterprises.

In the third place, Americans often appear to have been puzzled by the thought of Canadians finding anything fundamentally worrying or harmful in U.S. entertainments and other communications. Given that the success in Canada of U.S. cultural products can ultimately come only as the result of a Canadian demand, freely expressed, this puzzlement is easily understood. The United States, moreover, is the principal embodiment—and the principal propagator—of the contemporary civilization of the Western world. From so privileged and powerful a vantage point, it may be difficult to comprehend why another community—and a very similar one, at that—should be so strangely preoccupied. Such a perspective leads, again, to an unseemly suspicion that the Canadian concern is rooted in a vested, not a principled, interest.

Policymakers in Canada have not been entirely immune to the influence of at least some of these considerations. The argument that a liberal regime has no business interfering with the free flow of ideas has been especially telling. But Canadian policymakers have been conscious as well that the disparity in the sizes of the U.S. and Canadian cultural markets has put Canadian cultural producers at a disadvantage unless they are prepared to compete with the Americans by joining them—that is, by producing U.S.-style products that deal with U.S.-style themes. Even then, Canadians may confront distributive obstacles of the branch-plant sort. American-owned theater chains may be inhospitable to the marketing of Canadian films that speak only to the Canadian experience. American-owned television networks may be (understandably) happy with Canadian advertising but be (understandably) resistant to Canadian programming. And so on.

In this context, the dilemma of the nation-building policymaker is how to preserve the prerequisites of a liberal society while still ensuring that Canadians wishing to speak locally to themselves—that is, to the Canadian community about the Canadian experience—have at their disposal economically viable mechanisms for doing so. Squaring this circle has usually involved a combination of three policy principles: (1) no policy should deny Canadians access to such foreign communications as they are determined to receive,[23] (2) Canadian policies should therefore focus instead on the encouragement of indigenous cultural producers (strategies of exclusion, in other words, are not appropriate, but strategies that give economic advantage to internal Canadian initiatives assuredly are), and (3) a sustained effort must always be made to persuade the United States that priming cultural pumps is not like subsidizing economic enterprises but should be accepted instead as a reasonable manifestation of the legitimate nation-building obligations of the state. Such measures should not be regarded south of the border as appropriate targets for conventional economic retaliation or even for diplomatic protest.[24]

Canadian cultural policy initiatives have had a relatively long history, and from the start they have unavoidably touched on American interests—or at least have reflected the American fact. In radio broadcasting, for example, transmission interference from U.S. stations using the same broadcast frequencies as their Canadian counterparts generated negotiations between the two countries as early as 1924, although the U.S. authorities appear to have had difficulty within their own jurisdiction in enforcing compliance with the frequency-allocation agreements that ensued. About the same time there were growing concerns that the operators of Canadian stations were failing "to make good use of Canadian talent," and that the lack of an east-west Canadian radio communications system, when combined with "the increasing use of programs from the United States would have an injurious effect on Canadian unity." On one account, "the concern of many" was "that the possibility of cultural annexation by the United States had reached the proportions of a 'new national crisis.'"[25] A variety of royal commissions and parliamentary committees have been tasked over the years to examine the various dimensions of this problem. Such inquiries led to the creation in 1932 of the Canadian Radio Broadcasting Commission, which was succeeded in 1936 by the Canadian Broadcasting Corporation. The regulatory licensing authority for Canadian broadcasters has enjoyed a number of institutional manifestations over the years, but since 1968 it has been represented by the Canadian Radio-Television and Telecommunications Commission (CRTC), which, among other things, determines the Canadian content rules that govern the programming of Canadian radio and television broadcasters as well as the regulatory regime for Canadian cable companies and related program distributors.

A similar impetus underlay the establishment in 1939 of the National Film Board and its mandate to interpret Canada, through film, to both Canadians and audiences abroad. The same was true of the Canadian Film Development Corporation (Telefilm Canada), which was created as a crown corporation in 1968 "to foster and promote the development of a feature film industry in Canada" with the help of a small loan fund (initially Can$10 million). In 1951 a Royal Commission on National Development in the Arts, Letters and Sciences generated a report[26] that led in 1957 to the creation of the Canada Council, complete with an endowment that allows it to provide financial encouragement to the arts, humanities, and social sciences.[27]

In yet another area, the publication of Canadian books (particularly, but not solely, in the academic domain where Canadian markets are usually too small to be economically viable) has been financially supported not only by federal agencies like the Social Sciences and Humanities Research Council of Canada but also by a number of governments at the provincial level, notably those of Ontario and Quebec. Canadian immigration regulations have been used to impose hiring rules designed to ensure that universities conduct a thorough search for Canadian professorial recruits before having recourse to foreign nationals in attempting to fill their academic vacancies. This has been partly designed to ensure that Canadian citizens and permanent residents have preferred access to Canadian jobs, but it has also been aimed at encouraging the survival, in reasonable measure, of Canadian perspectives in the pedagogical and research operations of Canada's postsecondary educational institutions.[28]

At a more general level, incentives have been introduced through the taxation system to encourage advertisers to make use of Canadian rather than foreign periodicals. This is a strategy that has been the source of recurrent disputes with U.S. authorities, most recently in relation to the Canadian edition of *Sports Illustrated* but historically in response to the protests particularly of *Time* and *Reader's Digest*.[29]

The Politics of Economic Defense

But the nation-building policies that have aroused most opposition in the United States have been those associated with the economic rather than the cultural strain in Canadian nationalism. Such policies have often stimulated resistance from *within* Canada, too, because U.S. interests frequently have grateful clients, willing dependents, and enthusiastic partners on the Canadian side of the border. On occasion, the resulting combination of political pressures has defeated the policy entirely. A famous example was the first budget, in 1963, of the minority government of Lester B. Pearson. Pearson's minister of finance was Walter Gordon, an economic nationalist of the liberal (that is, private sector) school.[30] Acknowledging in his budget address the importance of foreign investment to Canadian prosperity, he nonetheless argued that the "extent of non-resident ownership and control" had gone "far beyond anything found in other countries in a comparable stage of industrial maturity." He thought accordingly that a greater degree of Canadian participation was appropriate, and foreign-owned firms ought to be encouraged to work toward achieving a minimum 25 percent Canadian equity interest in their Canadian operations. With this consideration in view, the budget reduced the 15 percent withholding tax payable on the dividends of private corporations to 10 percent in the case of companies owned 25 percent or more by Canadian residents but increased withholding to 20 percent in the case of companies that failed to meet this floor. In addition, the minister introduced a 30 percent tax "on certain sales by Canadian residents to non-residents and non-resident controlled companies, of shares in Canadian companies listed on Canadian stock exchanges." A 30 percent tax was also imposed on the sale by any listed Canadian corporation "of the whole or substantially the whole of its property" to a non-resident individual or company.[31]

Authorities in Washington were soon expressing criticism. But spokespersons for the financial community in Canada (the president of the Montreal and Canadian Stock Exchanges most vociferously among them) expressed not criticism but outrage, and they issued dire warnings about the probable impact of the initiative on the value of Canadian securities. The stock markets themselves were soon providing supportive evidence as wary traders voted with their money. Within six days, the government was forced to announce that the takeover tax would be withdrawn. Because the uproar continued at home and escalated south of the border, the withholding tax provisions were also watered down and were effectively abandoned in the following year.

In retrospect, the financial realities that so rudely confined the options of the Canadian government in 1963 provided a glimpse of a future that in another two decades would similarly confine the governments of some of the strongest economies in the developed world. From the perspective of economic nationalists, this was to be an inhospitable prospect—a future that would not work.

But such realities were not yet fully understood, and other measures were soon to be tried. From the U.S. point of view, Canada's creation of the Foreign Investment Review Agency (FIRA) and the National Energy Program (NEP) were probably among the most irritating. Established by the Liberal government of Pierre Elliott Trudeau in 1973 in the wake of yet another examination of the impact of foreign ownership on the Canadian economy,[32] FIRA's purpose was to screen not only foreign acquisitions of existing Canadian enterprises but also proposals for the creation of new businesses in Canada by foreign firms. In making its recommendations to the government, FIRA was to consider such factors as the effect of the investment on employment and economic activity generally, as well as on productivity, R&D, and product variety. It was also to assess the degree to which Canadians would participate in management, the effect of the investment on competition, and the investment's overall compatibility with Canadian national policies. In practice, however, FIRA was a paper tiger. Almost all applications were approved. But foreigners perceived it as discriminatory, and the business community in Canada did not like it either. In an irony of evolution, its mandate was changed in 1984 under the Progressive Conservative government of Brian Mulroney; henceforth it would promote rather than discourage investment from abroad, and its new purpose was to be conveyed by a new name: Investment Canada.

The NEP was considerably more complex but equally ill-fated. Stimulated by the dramatic increases in world oil prices that had followed the 1979 revolution in Iran, the NEP was introduced in 1980 and was composed of an intricate package of measures that were designed to affect not only domestic oil and gas prices (keeping them well below world levels) but also the pattern of demand and supply, the final distribution of revenues from production, and the ownership structure of the industry itself. To pay for the various measures involved, new taxes were introduced that had the effect of transferring income from both the energy companies and the producing provinces (notably Alberta but also Saskatchewan and British Columbia) to the federal government. Exploration for new sources of supply would be encouraged in the north with the help of a petroleum incentives program (PIP). Grants under the program would be distributed in a way that reflected the degree to which a firm could claim Canadian ownership. At the same time, some of the new tax revenue was to be made available to Petro-Canada (a government-owned petroleum company originally established in 1973) for the purchase of new acquisitions. The government also proposed to buy back foreign-owned firms and, even more controversially, to institute a "back-in" by which it would appropriate—both in the future and retroactively—a 25 percent interest in any oil and gas discovered on government lands (mainly in the north).[33]

The inevitable consequence was a phalanx of opposition mounted most vigorously by three categories of player: (1) the producing provinces (which saw themselves as the victims of a raid on their wealth inspired by the economic interests and political power of central and eastern Canada), (2) the multinational petroleum companies, and (3) the United States. Alberta went so far as to retaliate by reducing its oil production and challenging the federal authorities in the courts. Before long, Ottawa had to agree to alter the NEP's pricing and taxation provisions to allow domestic prices to move closer to world levels. Further adjustments followed in 1983 under the pressure of a decline in the world price of oil, a drop in the volume of gas exports to the United States, and an economic recession. The dismantling process continued after the election of the Progressive Conservative government in 1984, with the elimination, among other things, of the controversial 25 percent "back-in" provision. The 1988 Canada-U.S. Free Trade Agreement (CUFTA) administered the coup de grâce. Under it, Canada cannot charge Americans a higher price for Canadian energy exports than it charges Canadians. In times of shortage, moreover, it cannot restrict supplies to the United States any more severely than it restricts them at home.

It should be emphasized that these various public policy initiatives represent only a small sample of what in fact has been a complex array. An intricate tale, for example, could also be told in connection with the regulation and ownership of Canadian financial institutions—and here, too, CUFTA (later incorporated into the North American Free Trade Agreement, or NAFTA) has had a dismantling effect. Moreover, it can be argued more broadly that much of the history of Canada itself has been devoted to an attempt to build a viably distinctive political community in North America in defiance of the combined forces of geography and economics. The construction in the nineteenth century of the Canadian Pacific Railway and the formation in the twentieth of Trans-Canada Airlines (Air Canada since 1965) were enterprises born of precisely this sort of marriage of economics with politics. Even the development of so mundane a project as the Trans-Canada Highway was at bottom a nation-building initiative, it being impossible until the mid-1960s for a motorist to drive from one end of the country to the other on a paved road. Having to use U.S. highways to circumvent the Great Lakes was not necessarily a practical inconvenience, and much Canadian traffic still prefers the U.S. route. But having no choice in the matter was certainly undignified.

Initiatives of this latter sort, however, were not in themselves the cause of tribulations in the conduct of Canada-U.S. relations, which came partly from cultural policy, occasionally from foreign policy, but more fundamentally (as we have seen) from economic policy. And with reference in particular to the latter, the 1980s brought a profound change.

Imaginings Transformed

The surface manifestation of this change had to do with trade, but transformations of a much more fundamental sort were beneath the surface. These transformations bear on the most basic of the conceptions of the role of the state in society, and reflect forces of technology and economics so powerful and pervasive that they now appear (for the moment at least) to lie well beyond the ability of humanity to manage by deliberate means.

Among other things, the transformations have undermined the traditional public philosophy of Canadian elites—not because the latter (in government, at least) have had a change of heart, but because they have been led to a diminished assessment of their own capacities as economic and social engineers. What has happened in Canada may eventually occur elsewhere; but the Canadian case is farther advanced, and its evolution and character warrant reflection.

These preliminary observations may imply that yet another discussion of the intricacies of CUFTA and its NAFTA successor will follow. And so it will, at least in part, but not at a level of intricacy. For what is truly significant about NAFTA from the Canadian perspective is not what it does to the environment of North American trade (although this is important, too), but what the mere fact of its having been negotiated at all says about the change of attitude of those who govern Canada and of those others by whom Canada's governors, in their turn, are most deeply influenced. To establish the character of this change at its surface, it will be convenient to consider how the government in Ottawa evaluated the Canada-U.S. relationship in 1972 and to compare this evaluation with the government's views and behavior in the mid-1980s.

Following President Richard Nixon's August 1971 imposition of a 10 percent surcharge on all dutiable imports and the failure of Canadian representatives to secure (in time-honored fashion) an exemption for Canadian exporters,[34] the Trudeau government launched a review of Canada's relations with the United States. The result was a discussion paper issued through the Department of External Affairs in the autumn of 1972. Entitled "Canada-U.S. Relations: Options for the Future," it was devoted mainly to the military, political, economic, and cultural facets of the problem of continental "integration." Not surprisingly, it found the U.S. presence to be pervasive in all four areas. In response to this confirmation of a well-known reality, the paper's architects were led to define three broad options.[35]

1. Try "to maintain more or less our present relationship with the United States with a minimum of policy adjustment." This option was advanced only to be rejected because it carried the "risk that, in pursuing a purely pragmatic course, we may find ourselves drawn more closely into the U.S. orbit."

2. "[M]ove deliberatedly toward closer integration with the United States." This option was given the same reception as the first. In the past, close integration had been rejected not on

economic grounds but because it had been "judged to be inconsistent with Canada's desire to preserve a maximum degree of
independence." This remained the dominant view. In the current
environment the "probable economic costs and benefits...would
require careful calculation." But the "more fundamental issues"
were "clearly political," and it was "a moot question whether
[the] option, or any part of it, is politically tenable in the present
or any foreseeable climate of Canadian public opinion."

    3. Formulate "[a] comprehensive, long-term strategy to de-
velop and strengthen the Canadian economy and other aspects
of our national life and, in the process, to reduce the present
Canadian vulnerability." This option was the chosen course. In
concrete policy terms, it implied a strategy aimed at diversifying
Canada's economic activities abroad together with a renewed
emphasis on traditional nation-building policies at home.

    Thirteen years later, however, the government, having initi-
ated bilateral free trade discussions with the United States, was
vigorously in pursuit of Option 2. It is possible to argue, and
some in fact have argued, that this volte-face was a product of
the switch in 1984 to the Progressive Conservative government
of Brian Mulroney and that the decision to proceed was itself a
close call—the result of deliberations among a handful of individual players who might just as easily have decided on a different course.

    But it is a common failing of decision-makers in high places
to think of themselves as the architects of history when the more
frequent reality is that they are the unconscious transmitters of
powerful forces that lie outside themselves. The context in
which the Mulroney initiative was undertaken warrants at least
summary description.

    In 1983, as the Trudeau government was approaching its
end, the Department of External Affairs issued a paper in which,
while rejecting bilateral free trade across the board, it proposed
the negotiation of limited Canada-U.S. free trade arrangements
on a sector-by-sector basis.[36] The political implications of doing
so were hardly mentioned, and they enjoyed a fleeting reference
only for purposes of dismissal.

    Two years later, in making the case for comprehensive nego-
tiations leading to a more general free trade agreement, the
department again focused mainly on the economic argument. In
a brief reference to political issues, however, it suggested that
freer trade would "strengthen the economic fabric of the country; . . . reduce regional differences on the conduct of trade

policy; and . . . reinforce a growing sense of national confidence." A bilateral treaty, moreover, "could be a better guarantor of our sovereignty than the gradual uncontrolled drift toward integration now taking place. The possible adverse consequences can be managed by pursuing deliberate policies of strengthening cultural and other fields of endeavour which would bolster our national identity."[37] The argument in the 1972 white paper had thus been displaced by its exact antithesis.

There was "politics" here. By 1985, bilateral free trade with the United States had been supported repeatedly by the Economic Council of Canada. It had also been advocated in the United States by the Senate Committee on Foreign Affairs. It was among the most important of the recommendations advanced in the massive, three-volume report of the Royal Commission on the Economic Union and Development Prospects for Canada.[38] It reflected the testimony conveyed to the Commission by influential communicants all across the country. Free trade was supported by all of the provincial governments save that of the branch-plant heartland of Ontario, and even there the authorities were cross-pressured by the conflicting opinions of a divided economic constituency. For decades the Canadian Manufacturers' Association had been a protectionist voice, but to its surprise, it now found that the majority of its members favored a free trade initiative. So did the Canadian Federation of Independent Business. So did the think tanks. And so did the professional expositors of mainstream economics along with the dominant players in the public service. Canada's policy elites quite simply had changed their minds and, hence, their advocacies. Bilateral free trade was an idea whose political time had come.[39]

The immediate reasons for the switch were practical and, of these, the ones that received the greatest attention were economic. If Canadian enterprises were to enjoy the economies of scale that are essential to efficiency in an increasingly competitive world, they have to have ready and secure access to a market of substantial size. From time to time in the past the government had hoped that this would not necessarily imply dependence on the U.S. market in particular. Diversification of trading and investment relationships abroad could provide at least part of the answer.[40] But experience had shown that access to the common market being constructed by the Europeans was not a promising alternative, and Japan and the countries of the exploding Pacific Rim were proving themselves to be similarly problematic. The developing countries of the South might be more receptive in principle but had limited purchasing power. The U.S. prospect (which was also the easy prospect for Canadians used to operating in the cultural comfort of the North American environment) was therefore crucial. But that prospect was itself in potential jeopardy given the growth of protectionist dispositions in the U.S. Congress—dispositions that were greatly strengthened by the receptiveness of the apparatus for administering U.S. trade policy to the blandishments of constituents in pursuit of specific economic interests. To avoid the economic catastrophe that would follow if Canadians were denied access to the only market of continental size currently open to them, the trading relationship needed to be institutionalized. It would then be sustained by clear rules and reasonable guarantees. It was safer, certainly, to have it governed by explicit understandings consistently applied than by the kaleidoscopic vagaries of pressure group politics.

Among professional economists and government economic administrators, of course, there was also the thought that a full exposure to the weight of U.S. competition would in itself have a salutary effect on the efficiency of Canadian enterprises and, hence, on their competitiveness in the world at large. This implied that some of them might become casualties but that those that survived would be toughened up for effective economic combat in a globalizing world. Arguments that are rooted, like this one, in the assumption that it is sometimes useful to take instruction from hard knocks make poor fodder for public politics. Nonetheless, a conviction so powerfully grounded in long-standing traditions of orthodox economic theory served well enough to enhance both the internal confidence and the external enthusiasm with which sophisticated advocates of free trade pursued their cause. It is easy for elites to be tough-minded.

The initiative's hidden agenda also included an item bearing on the management of Canada's domestic economy. Canada's federation is relatively decentralized, and the jurisdictions over which the component provinces preside are substantial and impressive. One of the consequences has been that provincial governments have frequently deployed protectionist public policies of their own. Canada's domestic market, in other words, has not been entirely "free." From the point of view of political rationality at the provincial level, this reflects the practical exercise of power in the interests of the local constituencies to whom provincial authorities are responsible. From the point of view of economic rationality at the national level, it is a madness from which economic inefficiency must inevitably ensue. It makes Canadians as a whole poorer. (It may not, of course, make all Canadians *as individuals* poorer.) Given Canada's decentralized constitutional structure and the power of the political forces that thrive within it, solving the problem is not a task that can be reliably assigned either to the public political process or to intergovernmental bargaining. But a free trade agreement with the United States could put rules in place and economic forces in play that would compel a liberalization of the internal economy, too. The market would certainly discipline private firms; perhaps it could also discipline governments.

These two arguments—the first entailing a willingness to accept substantial private sector casualties in the interest of enhancing the efficiency of the economy as a whole and the second implying a comparable willingness to weaken the ability of provincial governments to protect their own economic communities at the expense of the national market—had at the time (and still have now) far-reaching implications for Canada's prevailing public philosophy. They amounted to an acceptance of the view that an important role of the state ought to be turned over to international market forces representing a kind of transnational invisible hand.

In matters of this sort, the facts often matter less than the premises, and the premises therefore warrant closer consideration. They go to the fundamentals.

The "peace, order, and good government" conservativism of Canada was a product in large measure of historical evolutions and accidents. For example, not every American wanted a revolution in 1776. Many of those who did not—the Loyalists—came to Canada, bringing with them their distrust of revolutionary exuberance and their confidence in the wisdom of sustaining the established order, monarchy and all. Their attitudes reinforced the political culture of what was eventually to become the Canadian state.

The survival, however, of the more conservative Canadian tradition was not simply a product of socialization, of generational hand-me-downs from the political preferences of a bygone era. It was the result, too, of an easy fit of attitudes with circumstance. There were fewer people in Canada. They were spread out in a long, thin line adjacent to the U.S. border. From the very beginning, the Europeans among them were divided into two

national parts. Diversities of language and custom were com-
pounded by diversities of other kinds—the most important of
them rooted in economics but rooted also in the distinctive histories, environments, and longevities of the provincial societies of
which Canada was eventually to be composed. The federal system was itself a manifestation of this reality, as were much of
Canadian public policy and much of Canadian political rhetoric.

Given this background, it is not surprising that Canadian
politicians have been known to speak of their country as a community of communities. In recent decades, entire government
departments have been established to serve the concept of a multicultural society and to promote the interests of its multicultural
components. And underlying this entire apparatus of attitudes,
values, and policies has been the assumption that the function of
the state is not only to provide an arena within which *individual*
citizens can safely pursue their personal destinies but also to sustain the security of *communities* of citizens in the places they re-
side. The national community operates at only one level, and
other levels are equally crucial to the conduct of a rewarding life.
It follows that the obligations of the state—even in matters economic—are far more intricate than the mere obligation to provide a responsible display of macroeconomic management. In
particular, obligations include the sustenance of a reasonable
measure of economic prosperity at the local, provincial, and regional community levels, even where such measures require acceptance of a less efficient economic structure than the national-
market-operated-by-competing-individuals model would generate.

A clear-cut example of what is at issue here can be easily
contrived by imagining the circumstances of a francophone resi-
dent of Quebec who, in midcareer, discovered that further professional pursuits required a move to rural Alberta. The
language in common use there would be different than in Quebec, as would be the educational traditions practiced in local
schools. So also perhaps would be the predominant local reli-
gions, the social life, and the popular entertainments. Discomfort—even alienation—could ensue. (In such circumstances, it
often does ensue.)

The underlying Canadian premise (fortified by the federal
structure and sustained by the realities of electoral politics and
interest articulation) is that this is a discomfort, or an alienation,
that Canadian citizens should not have to face simply because of

economic circumstances. It follows that government has an important obligation to try to ensure that local economies work—that is, that they are prosperous enough to make it unnecessary for community-committed citizens to move great distances to find employment. Individuals find meaning in their lives by many routes, and one of the most important comes from ongoing enjoyment of the local society of which they are a part. If the economy operates in such a way as to deprive them of this source of fulfillment, and if the state makes no attempt to countervail the economy's impact, individual citizens may end up economically richer and professionally more powerful[41] but socially, culturally, and psychologically poorer. That, in turn, may lead to community decay of other kinds, among them the loss of community supports for neighbors who have come on hard times, the uprooted urbanite's despairing sense of isolated anonymity, and, in the extreme, the proliferation of crime and other manifestations of indifference to obligation.

This argument is easily understood in the case of the francophone transplanted to rural Alberta. But the same phenomenon also applies to Newfoundlanders transplanted to Toronto, Cape Bretoners transplanted to Vancouver, and so on. It explains why they so often return "home" to retire, and why it is often so difficult to persuade even the poorest of them to go "down the road" in the first place.[42] Communities count.

From this perspective, the true significance of CUFTA lies more in the decision to negotiate it than in the substance of its provisions because it reflected an abandonment of received philosophy of Canadian governance. The makers of Canadian public policy were saying, in effect, that they no longer had sufficient faith in the community maintenance economic policies of the state to continue to support them in the face of impersonal, but intensifying, market forces. Part of this argument was technical. Ottawa could not appear to make Newfoundland (for example) economically prosperous on the basis of known strategies for stimulating economic growth. And it could no longer afford to sustain such communities as Newfoundland represents by simple income redistribution mechanisms.[43] Perhaps the market could do a better job. If it failed, then it rather than the government would be the purveyor of the bad news—of the requirements that more labor become more mobile and that communities be regarded as secondary to the rational conduct of economic life. What communities have to offer, according to this view, is not a primary value. What matters is the satisfaction of individual appetites by material means and the growth of the taxable national product.

None of this is intended to suggest that this new view is necessarily the wrong view. Perhaps it is. Perhaps it is not. In any case, it is too early to tell. But it is certainly a departure from past practice, and it amounts to the acceptance of that liberal materialist conception of the good life and the good society that is an inherent feature of the process of economic globalization. Canadian policymakers, in effect, have bought into a pattern of forces that they can no longer resist. A handful have complained,[44] but most of them have not, and a surprising number show signs of being unable to understand why what they are doing might be perceived by others as problematic. They are losing the capacity to identify the question.

This evolution did not come entirely without warning. Of course, any careful student of political philosophy, social theory, or modern literature can point to a long succession of intellectual signposts on the road to modernity and can find articulate expression of many a hesitation en route. But in Canada, and in the context particularly of Canadian nationalist responses to the United States as the principal custodian of the modern worldview, the most prominent and powerful of the analysts of change was probably George Grant. A conservative philosopher—but not a conservative of the U.S. kind—he argued in the early 1960s that Canada is ultimately doomed as a distinctive political experiment (it might survive, but not distinctively) because its ruling elites have come to accept, and to accommodate, the U.S. version of the liberal idea—a version that, given its roots in the European Enlightenment of the eighteenth century and, even earlier, in the epistemology of the scientific revolution, sanctifies the idea of progress through technique. Ideas, for Grant, are causally fundamental: they determine political and economic structures. It is not the other way around. From ideas come our conceptions of justice, our understanding of what constitutes a good society, and even our notions of what it means to say we "know." The U.S. idea has been tried—with almost ruthless efficiency—in a land of boundless opportunity and with a minimum of opposition. In such circumstances, the U.S. idea has reinforced itself and has acquired an enormous store of the assets of power. It is suffused with optimism and is expressed in the belief that the environment can be usefully manipulated and exploited at will with the right combination of hard work and effective engineering, whether material or social. There being no internalized experience of defeat, there is no hesitation, no sense that the adversities of history usually win. So powerful is the U.S. example, and so pervasive its means of propagation, that Canadians—even the *Canadiens* of Acadia and Quebec—have come gradually to shed their more organic understandings of society and to share the U.S. view. In fact, those who occupy seats of power in Canada have become so fully transformed that they have ceased even to understand the community that their predecessors sought to defend. In such circumstances—reflecting a kind of unintended takeover of the mind—there is little to do but grieve the final departure of the Canadian alternative.[45] There is a sense in which what Grant, with his prescience, saw in the mid-1960s became visible to everyone in the 1980s. But by then the powerful did not notice—or did not care.

Consequences

This observation leads to the conclusion of this essay, for the fact of the matter is that the successful conclusion of the bilateral free trade negotiations with the United States, even more than the NAFTA negotiations that followed them, signaled the end (for the time being, at least) of any explicit Canadian nationalism in a form that could reasonably be of serious concern to Americans. There was for a time a repercussive rhetoric among intellectuals, artists, trade unions, and the entrepreneurial casualties of U.S. competition; but even among these there is now the powerful sense of a battle lost. It is accompanied by signs of fatalistic resignation. The special nationalism of Quebec still survives, of course, and it will continue to survive in spite of the defeat of the 1995 sovereignty referendum. It will also survive the defeat of the next such referendum (should a defeat be once again the result). But whatever the outcome, Quebecois nationalism sees itself as a friend of the United States and will not threaten the economic, much less the security, interests of the American Republic. Those who pursue the independence of Quebec now feel crimped, not by liberal modernity but by the power- and office-sharing requirements of Canadian federalism. If they are successful in their quest to replace the need for constant compromise within Canada with the need for constant compromise outside it, they will be quick to convey reassurances to their southern neighbor and to the custodians of its capital.

In the meantime, in Canada as a whole the search for identity—for a national raison d'être capable of distinguishing the Canadian from the U.S. experiment—focuses on purely internal matters expressed through internal policy. Canadians have Medicare, and by such means do they manifest their sense of community—their sense of themselves as compassionate in adversity. Canadians have recently been told that they must now register their guns—*all* of them—and exotic firearms have become, in the past few weeks, more tightly controlled than ever before. By these new regulations, Canadians may—or may not— reduce the already modest level of violence in their society, but they will be acting in concert with their love of peace, order, and good government, and in this, they will certainly distinguish themselves (symbolically, at least) from Americans.

In skeptical response to this reassuring assertion, Americans might be moved to point to disputes on the current Canada-U.S. agenda—disputes over softwood lumber, the Pacific salmon fishery, the accessibility of Canadian cable systems for the producers of U.S. country music television programming, the marketing system in Canada for dairy and poultry products and wheat, the economic operations of Canadian firms in Cuba, and so on. But even to list such issues is to recognize that in most cases the real stakes are relatively small and that in only one or two (on the Cuban issue especially) is there even a hint of a nationalist preoccupation. These are the kinds of questions that crop up in conventional politics everywhere—as much within states as between them. In the Pacific salmon dispute, for example, the quarrel with Alaskan fishermen appears to have been as vigorously mounted in the states of Washington and Oregon as in the province of British Columbia. The softwood lumber dispute seems never to end, but this is due more to the repetitive appeals of the U.S. lumber industry against the findings of institutionalized dispute settlement mechanisms than to any conflict of nationalities. The country music dispute had its origins in the desire of the CRTC to guarantee room on Canadian cable networks for Canadian performers, a long-standing Commission policy; in any case the issue was ultimately resolved by an agreement that allowed the U.S. distributor to purchase a 20 percent interest in its Canadian competitor. These, in short, are the kinds of issues to which solutions are nearly always found. They are the routine stuff of routine politics, and they are bound to recur. They are not about nationalism but about interest. The fact that the players involved include two sovereign states is almost incidental.

In these circumstances—circumstances in which Canadians have come fundamentally to share the most significant of the premises underlying the U.S. worldview—it is hard to avoid an obvious conclusion: if Americans have difficulty working with Canada, they will have difficulty working with any external sovereignty. If they find Canadians even mildly troublesome, puzzling, or inconvenient, they will find other nationalities unfathomable. For in Canada (at least in areas that matter to the United States), Americans have largely won over the prevailing public philosophy and, with it, the rules of the game. All that remains for the Canada-U.S. relationship is Yankee trading, and Yankee trading can hardly be alien to Americans. Excitable members of the Congress—Mr. Helms not least among them—should relax. One of the prerequisites, after all, for enjoying a victory is knowing when you have won.

A final observation needs to be made. What Canadians have experienced through the diffusion of the U.S. conception of liberal modernity is increasingly being experienced elsewhere. And elsewhere, too, it excites a comparable anxiety and a comparably ambiguous response. The vehicle for the dissemination on an international scale of the ideas entailed in the pursuit of happiness, as Americans have come to understand them, is the international marketplace, fortified by technology and the process of globalization. But this process represents a challenge to community *everywhere*. In a world in which even the French—the confident custodians of a culture that they think has no peer—are frightened by death stars, the intensity of the disturbance that emanates from an impersonal modernity that is indifferent to difference cannot be denied. It is this reality that creates the paradox of a world hurtling toward functional integration while its component populations cling to romantic conceptions of the sovereign state as the ideal embodiment of group identity. Their clinging to the idea of polity is the response of their communal imagination to the atomistic homogenization of their material world.

In the end, the Canadian dilemma in North America is the contemporary dilemma of community itself.

Notes

1. John W. Holmes, "Nationalism in Canadian Foreign Policy," *Nationalism in Canada*, ed. Peter Russell (Toronto: McGraw-Hill, 1966), 204.

2. This may seem to Americans to be an unpardonably partisan assertion, and I am fully aware that we are dealing here with a perpetually interactive relationship in which the question of "who started what, when" is almost always open to debate. I hope, however, that the point will become clear as the discussion proceeds.

3. See Benedict Anderson, *Imagined Communities: Reflections on the Origin and Spread of Nationalism* (New York: Verso, 1991).

4. In Isaiah Berlin, "The Bent Twig: A Note on Nationalism," *Foreign Affairs* 51, no. 1 (October 1972): 17.

5. The two world wars were cataclysms, certainly, but the first was fought in defense of the British Empire, and, even in the second, Canadians could hardly claim to have been the leading players. The Great Depression was a cataclysm of another kind, but it, too, was an experience shared with others. Only among Quebecois, it can be argued, has there been a truly "defining moment"—their defeat at the hands of the British in 1759. And with that assertion, First Nations, *Acadians*, *Métis*, and other particularities might still be inclined to quarrel. In Canada, even the benchmark traumas of history have a pluralist distribution.

6. According to the RCMP, the agreement with Walt Disney Co. (Canada) Ltd. "will help finance community police work threatened by federal budget cuts." Disney "will manage and administer the licensing for all RCMP-related merchandise on behalf of the Mounted Police Foundation, a registered charity that holds the rights to RCMP intellectual property." Royalties, expected to reach Can$25 million over the five years of the agreement, will be divided between the company and the foundation. See Harvey Enchin, "Nothing Goofy about RCMP Deal," *Globe and Mail* (Toronto), June 29, 1995, p. B1.

7. Margaret Atwood, *Survival: A Thematic Guide to Canadian Literature* (Toronto: Anansi, 1972). As a thematic interpretation of Canada's literature, Atwood's thesis is obviously open to argument. Its significance, however, lies less in the accuracy of the literary portrait it conveys than in its resonance with Canadian readers.

8. Not all Canadians would agree, and some find much to reward them in the modesty of their myths, which they like to think are a good match for their virtues. For an engaging exploration of these themes by an accomplished and popular expositor of the Canadian experience and identity, see Pierre Berton, *Why We Act Like Canadians: A Personal Exploration of Our National Character* (Toronto: McClelland & Stewart, 1982). The discussion is offered in the format of a series of "Letters to an American Friend" and, like so many Canadian disquisitions on this subject, attempts to define the Canadian reality by contrasting it with the American.

Among the best of the more scholarly treatments at this level of analysis are those of the U.S. political sociologist, Seymour Martin Lipset. See especially his *Continental Divide: The Values and Institutions of the United States and Canada* (New York: Routledge, 1990). A stimulating series of recent inquiries into similar themes by scholars in Canada can be found in

David Thomas, ed., *Canada and the United States: Differences that Count* (Peterborough, Ont.: Broadview Press, 1993).

Edgar Z. Friedenberg, a thoughtful American émigré to Canada who is best known for his radical critiques of the educational establishment, tried some years ago to come to grips with the differences between the American and Canadian approaches to authority. See his *Deference to Authority: The Case of Canada* (White Plains, N.Y.: M. E. Sharpe, 1980).

Allan Smith, a Canadian historian, considers these and similar themes in his *Canada—An American Nation? Essays on Continentalism, Identity, and the Canadian Frame of Mind* (Montreal & Kingston: McGill-Queen's University Press, 1994). The common notion that Canada is culturally more pluralistic than the United States is challenged by Jeffrey G. Reitz and Raymond Breton in *The Illusion of Difference: Realities of Ethnicity in Canada and the United States* (Toronto: C. D. Howe Institute, 1994). A lively presentation of a wide array of statistical indicators of the similarities and contrasts in Canadian and U.S. life can be found in Roger Sauve, *Borderlines* (Toronto: McGraw-Hill Ryerson, 1994).

9. Americans wishing to consult a more extensive but still very manageable guide to the Canadian nationalist literature of this period should investigate Sylvia B. Bashevkin, *True Patriot Love: The Politics of Canadian Nationalism* (Toronto: Oxford University Press, 1991). See especially chapter 1, "Exploring the Nationalist World View," 1–38.

10. James M. Minifie, *Peacemaker or Powder-Monkey: Canada's Role in a Revolutionary World* (Toronto: McClelland & Stewart, 1960), 3–5.

11. Peyton V. Lyon, *The Policy Question: A Critical Appraisal of Canada's Role in World Affairs* (Toronto: McClelland & Stewart, 1963). The argument for maintaining "diplomatic credit" is developed in Chapter 2, "Canada's Diplomatic Assets," 22–40. The rejoinder to the argument for neutralism is in chapter 4, "The Role for Canada," 54–78.

12. James M. Minifie, *Open at the Top: Reflections on U.S.-Canada Relations* (Toronto: McClelland and Stewart, 1964).

13. Stephen Clarkson, *An Independent Foreign Policy for Canada?* (Toronto: McClelland and Stewart, 1968).

14. A.D.P. Heeney and Livingston T. Merchant, *Canada and the United States: Principles for Partnership*, June 28, 1965, 48–50. The working group's terms of reference are in Annex A.

15. The first book-length presentation of this view appeared somewhat later and reflected information contained in the so-called Pentagon Papers. See Charles Taylor, *Snow Job: Canada, the United States and Vietnam (1954 to 1973)* (Toronto: Anansi, 1974).

16. This is, of course, an oversimplified summation. The argument can be found in fully elaborated form in Stephen Clarkson's conclusion to *An Independent Foreign Policy for Canada?* His chapter has the subtitle, "The Choice to be Made." See 253–269.

17. The seminars, however, which were attended from time to time by members of the Canadian foreign service, stimulated an internal review of the premises of Canadian policy. The review was conducted during the final

months of the Liberal government of Lester B. Pearson. See Bruce Thordarson, *Trudeau and Foreign Policy: A Study in Decision-Making* (Toronto: Oxford University Press, 1972), 111–112; and J. L. Granatstein and Robert Bothwell, *Pirouette: Pierre Trudeau and Canadian Foreign Policy* (Toronto: University of Toronto Press, 1990), 10–11.

18. It should be noted that in foreign policy generally Canadian governments have tended to favor the standard tactical repertoires of the weak in dealing with the strong. Hence, they have preferred to operate whenever possible in institutionalized multilateral environments and have tried to diversify their international relationships. In dealing more directly with the United States, they have also shown a preference for dealing with one issue at a time. Linkage is not usually in the interest of the underdog.

19. This does not mean that the relationship was without noisy incident. One of the most famous of these occurred as the result of a speech by Prime Minister Pearson at Temple University on April 2, 1965, in which he called for "a suspension of air strikes against North Vietnam." President Johnson immediately invited him to lunch at Camp David, where Johnson subjected his hapless visitor to a tirade: "You don't," Johnson said, "come here and piss on my rug." John English, *The Worldly Years: The Life of Lester Pearson, 1949–1972* (Toronto: Alfred A. Knopf Canada, 1992), 364.

The "quiet" of quiet diplomacy is occasionally relieved by representations publicly made, but it is unusual in the Canadian-U.S. context for public representations to lead to such raucous reactions, even in private. This episode preceded, of course, the Clarkson seminars.

20. For an excellent review, see J.L. Granatstein, "Free Trade Between Canada and the United States: The Issue That Will Not Go Away," in *The Politics of Canada's Economic Relationship with the United States,* Denis Stairs and Gilbert R. Winham, eds., (Toronto: University of Toronto Press in cooperation with the Royal Commission on the Economic Union and Development Prospects for Canada and the Canadian Government Publishing Centre, Supply and Services Canada, 1985), 11–54.

21. The literature bearing on these various themes was being produced in this period at an impressive rate. Much of it originated with a group of academicians based largely in Ontario, many of them associated with the University of Toronto. Several books of essays emerged from the same series of seminars that had spawned Stephen Clarkson's *An Independent Foreign Policy for Canada?* Among them were Abraham Rotstein, ed., *The Prospect of Change: Proposals for Canada's Future* (Toronto: McGraw-Hill, 1965); Peter Russell, ed., *Nationalism in Canada* (Toronto: McGraw-Hill, 1966); and Ian Lumsden, ed., *Close the 49th Parallel, etc.: The Americanization of Canada* (Toronto: University of Toronto Press, 1970). Rotstein remained for many years the most active and thoughtful exponent of the nationalist position. Perhaps the most instructive of his many essays are those contained in his *The Precarious Homestead: Essays on Economics, Technology and Nationalism* (Toronto: new press, 1973).

For a useful collection of contemporary readings drawn from government reports as well as from independent sources, see Abraham

Rotstein and Gary Lax, eds., *Independence: The Canadian Challenge* (Toronto: Committee for an Independent Canada, 1972). One of the most influential studies of the day was Kari Levitt, *Silent Surrender: The Multinational Corporation in Canada* (Toronto: Macmillan, 1970). The process by which some of the academics were led to political activism by their academic research is illuminated in Dave Godfrey and Mel Watkins, eds., *Gordon to Watkins to You—A Documentary: the Battle for Control of our Economy* (Toronto: new press, 1970). A bibliography of treatments by orthodox economists can be found in A.E. Safarian, *Foreign Ownership of Canadian Industry* (Toronto: McGraw-Hill, 1966). The reasoning of a Liberal politician and chartered accountant who became seized with the issue of foreign ownership is outlined in Walter L. Gordon, *A Choice for Canada: Independence or Colonial Status* (Toronto: McClelland and Stewart, 1966). In attempting to deal with the foreign ownership phenomenon in his capacity as minister of finance during the early years of the government of Lester B. Pearson, Mr. Gordon had already had a rough ride. We will return to his experience below.

22. Several were involved in task forces for the government. Some became active in nationalist pressure groups like the Committee for an Independent Canada. A few were very heavily involved in an organized attempt to persuade the New Democratic Party to adopt a more vigorous version of the economic nationalist position.

23. There have been occasional exceptions. For example, the private use of dish antennae to pick up satellite television transmissions was for some years illegal in Canada. But the regulation had about as much success as prohibition, and the government eventually gave up. Enforcement problems aside, one of the difficulties was that the prohibition was unfair. Canadians who lived close to the Canada-U.S. border could receive all the U.S. broadcasts they wished, and only those who resided farther north felt the full brunt of the prohibition. Technology and liberalism go together in more ways than one.

24. The flavor of the Canadian position can be found in dozens of reports and private studies. The most important of them are reviewed in Bashevkin, *True Patriot Love*, chapter 1. Almost all of them struggle with the question of how to respond to the nation-building requirement without violating either the liberal philosophical premise or the sensitivities of the United States. One of the clearest expositions is contained in Royal Commission on Broadcasting, *Report* (Ottawa: Queen's Printer and Controller of Stationery, March 15, 1957). See especially chapter 1, pp. 8–9, entitled simply "The Problem."

To illustrate, after observing that a single television station in Chicago could reach a market equal to that of all 38 television stations then established across Canada, the commission went on to observe the following:

> The central, unique fact about Canadian broadcasting is that we are here in North America, a nation of 16 million people living beside a nation of 168 million which speaks the language of our majority and is rich, inventive, with a highly developed broadcasting system of its own. No other country is similarly helped and embarrassed by

the United States. Much that is good and valuable can come from this closeness. . . .

But as a nation we cannot accept, in these powerful and persuasive media, the natural and complete flow of another nation's culture without danger to our national identity. Can we resist the tidal wave of American cultural activity? Can we retain a Canadian identity, art and culture—a Canadian nationhood? These questions do not imply a judgment on the values of the American broadcasting system; indeed, the dangers to Canadian national identity are much greater from the good American programs than from their poor or clumsy productions. Assuming, as we must, that their broadcasting system is satisfactory and suitable for Americans, this is no basis for thinking it is desirable for Canadians. . . .

Nor is this attitude in Canada antagonistic to the United States— a form of anti-Americanism which most Canadians would resist and deplore. The same attitude would apply equally to the flooding of Canada by cultural influences from the United Kingdom or France. It is only the accident of geography and the technology of broadcasting that make the threat to our national identity greater from the United States. . . .

. . . we were interested when we visited the United States to find that there are thoughtful Americans who feel that the United States will be enriched by the preservation of a separate and distinct cultural identity in Canada.

25. Royal Commission on Broadcasting, *Report*, Appendix II: "A Brief History of Broadcasting in Canada," 298–299.

26. Royal Commission on National Development in the Arts, Letters and Sciences, *Report* (Ottawa: Queen's Printer, 1951).

27. The academic mission of the Canada Council was reassigned in 1978 to the newly created Social Sciences and Humanities Research Council of Canada. The Canada Council's mandate is now largely confined to the arts.

28. The controversy over the extent of U.S. influence in Canadian universities can be explored in a collection of readings edited by Robin Mathews and James Steele, *The Struggle for Canadian Universities* (Toronto: new press, 1969).

29. The tale is told in detail in Isaiah Litvak and Christopher Maule, *Cultural Sovereignty: The Time and Reader's Digest Case in Canada* (New York: Praeger, 1974).

30. To the extent that Gordon's views were informed by his experience as a chartered accountant in the industrial and financial heartland of Toronto and its environs, he came by them honestly. His life is recounted in Denis Smith, *Gentle Patriot: A Political Biography of Walter Gordon* (Edmonton: Hurtig, 1973). The story of the budget and its repercussions is told from Gordon's point of view in chapters 7 and 8. See also Charlotte S. M. Girard, *Canada in World Affairs, Vol. XIII: 1963–1965* (Toronto: Canadian Institute of International Affairs, 1979), 100–109. For the prime minister's perspective, see John A. Munro and Alex I. Inglis, eds., *Mike: The Memoirs of the Rt. Hon.*

Lester B. Pearson—Volume 3: 1957–1968 (Toronto: University of Toronto Press, 1975), 103–110.

31. Girard, *Canada in World Affairs*, 101–102.

32. The report was leaked and can be found under the title "A Citizen's Guide to the Herb Gray Report: Domestic Control of the National Economic Environment," *Canadian Forum* 51 (December 1971).

33. The story of the NEP is summarily recounted in the context of Canadian-U.S. relations in this period more generally by J.L. Granatstein and Robert Bothwell in their *Pirouette*, especially chapter 12, "Welcome to the 1980s," (311–335). See also Stephen Clarkson, *Canada and the Reagan Challenge: Crisis in the Canadian-American Relationship* (Toronto: Canadian Institute for Economic Policy, 1982), chapter 3, "The National Energy Program and Canadianization." For more detail, see Bruce Doern and Glen Toner, *The Politics of Energy: The Development and Implementation of the NEP* (Toronto: Methuen, 1985). A recent assessment is in Christina McCall and Stephen Clarkson, *Trudeau and Our Times—Volume 2: The Heroic Delusion* (Toronto: McClelland & Stewart, 1994), especially chapter 5, "The National Energy Program and National Disunity."

34. It has been quite common for U.S. legislators and administrators, in hot pursuit of economic targets overseas, to make use of measures that have the unintended effect of side-swiping Canada. In such circumstances, Canadian representatives normally seek an exemption, and their representations are frequently rewarded.

35. Mitchell Sharp, "Canada-U.S. Relations: Options for the Future," in *International Perspectives—Special Issue* (Ottawa: External Affairs Canada, Autumn 1972). The options themselves are explored on pp. 13–24.

36. Department of External Affairs, *Canadian Trade Policy for the 1980s: A Discussion Paper* (Ottawa: Minister of Supply and Services Canada, 1983). The paper was accompanied by a more substantial volume entitled *A Review of Canadian Trade Policy: A Background Document to Canadian Trade Policy for the 1980s* (Ottawa: Minister of Supply and Services Canada, 1983). In its substance, the proposal was a nonstarter because it could not have been of serious interest to the U.S. authorities.

37. Minister for International Trade and Secretary of State for External Affairs, *Canadian Trade Negotiations: Introduction, Selected Documents, Further Reading* (Ottawa: Department of External Affairs, December 15, 1985), 32.

38. See the three-volume *Report of the Royal Commission on the Economic Union and Development Prospects for Canada* (Ottawa: Minister of Supply and Services Canada, 1985). Vol. I is the most pertinent.

39. Not everyone would agree, of course, with this interpretation, and the literature on both the Canada-U.S. and the North American free trade agreements is voluminous. Those who wish to understand more fully the politics of the Canada-U.S. agreement from the Canadian side should consult the two most substantial accounts that have appeared thus far. See G. Bruce Doern and Brian W. Tomlin, *Faith and Fear: The Free Trade Story* (Toronto: Stoddart, 1991), and Michael Hart, with Bill Dymond and Colin Robertson, *Decision at Midnight: Inside the Canada-U.S. Free-Trade Negotiations* (Vancouver: UBC Press, 1994). Hart, a foreign service officer, played an important role in the initiative. It is safe to say, however, that the final assessment is not yet in.

40. "Contractual links" were thus negotiated with the European Community and later with Japan in the middle 1970s. Neither came to much.

41. Even this, of course, applies for the most part only to citizens of the middle and upper-middle classes. The community to which professionals belong is often the profession itself, or the firm. But professionals—economists among them—make a mistake when they extend the premise of their own lives to everyone else. For most people, work has a bad name for a good reason.

42. The phrase comes from the title of a 1970 Canadian film, *Goin' Down the Road*, that was admired especially for its gritty authenticity. It tells the story of some youths from Cape Breton who "go down the road" to Toronto in happy search of fortune; however, their exposure to an indifferent city serves only to destroy them.

43. Whether it *really* could no longer afford to do this is itself, of course, a matter for argument. Some would say that the claim has less to do with capacity than with will and that the "will" of the richer parts of the country to prolong the existing arrangements had simply run out. There were also concerns that traditional policies were creating psychological attitudes of dependency that are inimical to the cultivation of incentive. The real motivation probably reflected a fortuitous conjunction of managerial loss of faith with a genuine fear of macroeconomic decline at a time of escalating taxes and accumulating public debt.

44. Among them are some of the members of the old guard associated with the postwar Department of External Affairs. For the flavor of their lament, see Arthur Andrew, *The Rise and Fall of a Middle Power: Canadian Diplomacy from King to Mulroney* (Toronto: James Lorimer, 1993), especially chapters 10–12.

45. A popular version of George Grant's argument can be found in his small book entitled *Lament for a Nation: The Defeat of Canadian Nationalism* (Toronto: McClelland and Stewart, 1965). His ideas are developed in more sophisticated form, however, in a series of essays collected under the title, *Technology and Empire: Perspectives on North America* (Toronto: House of Anansi, 1969). For the philosophical underpinnings of his position, see his *Philosophy in the Mass Age* (Toronto: Copp Clark, 1959); *Time as History* (Toronto: Canadian Broadcasting Corporation, 1969); and *English-Speaking Justice* (Sackville, N.B.: Mount Allison University, 1974). The latter includes a critical assessment of the contemporary philosopher of liberalism, John Rawls.

Much illumination can be obtained from placing Grant's thought in the context of the ideas of two other formidable Canadian thinkers, Marshall McLuhan and Harold Innis. This task has been undertaken in magnificent style by Arthur Kroker in his *Technology and the Canadian Mind: Innis/McLuhan/Grant* (Montreal: New World Perspectives, 1984).

2

Canada and Economic Sovereignty

Murray G. Smith

At the end of the twentieth century, it seems ironic that the end of the cold war, the global shift toward more market-oriented economic policies, and the international spread of democracy have been accompanied by a resurgence of interest in and concern about sovereignty. The original meaning of sovereignty was the authority or prerogatives of the monarch, yet modern democratic states have assumed these prerogatives and guard them jealously.

For many nations, concern about sovereignty is associated with territorial integrity. A nation such as Poland, for example, which has been repeatedly invaded and whose boundaries have shifted, understandably may have lingering anxieties about its territorial integrity.

Canadian concerns about sovereignty have some distinctive features. Indeed, Canada is a monarchy. The head of state is also queen of the United Kingdom, which sometimes raises symbolic sovereignty questions for foreign observers. The monarchy, however, is not a significant political issue; it is simply accepted as part of the woodwork despite the fact that Canada is perennially preoccupied by constitutional questions. The main significance of this historical vestige is that it is associated with the British parliamentary form of government that has evolved in Canada since the 1790s without the revolutionary ruptures that created the American and French republics.

Canada does not face significant external threats to its territorial integrity.[1] The main challenges to its territorial integrity come from within in the form of the continuing debate about sovereignty for Quebec and the claims of aboriginal peoples.

Canadian concerns about sovereignty in the last half of the twentieth century have focused on the questions of economic, political, and cultural independence in the context of increased economic integration, questions that are now gripping other nations and societies, including the United States. Yet Canadian concerns about sovereignty have changed during the last 30 years.

In the 1960s and 1970s, Canadian concerns about economic, political, and cultural sovereignty were focused on anxieties about the high level of foreign ownership of the economy and the unregulated export of natural resource products, which were perceived as being sold too cheaply to foreigners. Canada attempted to address these anxieties through the use of government subsidies and the establishment of crown (government-owned) corporations.

The anxieties about resource dependence and foreign domination of the economy persisted in some form until recently and were prominent features of the Canadian debate about free trade with the United States. However, the thesis of this paper is that economic nationalism has waned in Canada and that the restructuring of the Canadian economy during the last two decades has contributed to this development. At the same time, these anxieties persist in specific areas such as the cultural industries, and political sensitivities associated with the sovereignty movement in Quebec continue.

Some Historical Reflections

During the first part of the nineteenth century, the United Kingdom provided preferential access to markets for the Canadian colonies. Then, in 1846, Britain unilaterally adopted free trade. Alarmed by the loss of Imperial Preferences, the Canadian colonies entered into a reciprocity treaty with the United States in 1854. This allowed free trade in a wide range of primary products. The treaty was for a term of 10 years, with a one-year notification requirement for termination.[2] As John Young observes:

> Particular bitterness was aroused in the United States by the Canadian tariff increases of 1858 and 1859. Since these involved manufactured goods, they were within the letter of the treaty, but it was argued that they were contrary to the spirit of the arrangement. Partly because of these increases, but mainly as a result of ill-feeling generated during the Civil War, the United States government abrogated the treaty at the first available opportunity, and the treaty ceased to be effective as of March, 1866.[3]

After confederation in 1867, Canada sought to renew the reciprocity treaty. Various attempts were made to reach a new agreement, but when the U.S. Senate failed to ratify the draft treaty of 1874, these attempts languished.

As a result Canada turned inward with the National Policy of 1879, which imposed high tariffs on imports. Canada continued efforts, however, to open trade with the United States, but these subsequent efforts to return to the reciprocity treaty also were rebuffed by the U.S. Congress.

Of course, not all of the problems were on the U.S. side; in 1911 a reciprocity treaty was ratified by the U.S. Senate but was rejected by Canada after an intense debate in a national election. The resounding defeat of the Liberal government of the day was taken as an expression of public opinion against freer trade with the United States. The campaign against the reciprocity treaty involved both economic nationalism and appeals to fervent patriotism for the Imperial connection.

It was not until 1935 that Canada and the United States negotiated and implemented a bilateral trade agreement. In 1948, a Canada-U.S. free trade agreement was discussed at some length, but the discussions ended when the Canadian prime minister, W.L. Mackenzie King, expressed his disapproval, allegedly because of concern about ties to Britain and the challenges of dairy policy.

Until World War II, the United Kingdom was Canada's most important trading partner. In 1938, for example, 40 percent of Canada's exports went to that country while only 23 percent went to the United States. After the war, the United Kingdom's importance as a market for Canadian exports declined steadily and finally fell to very low levels after that country entered the European Community (EC).

The decisive switch in Canadian trade policy perspective came when Canada became a signatory to the General Agreement on Tariffs and Trade (GATT) in 1947. This committed Canada, at least grudgingly, to an outward-looking policy of multilateral trade liberalization. From 1947 to 1960 several rounds of negotiations accomplished small reductions in tariffs. Then, in 1963, came the Kennedy Round, at which negotiators agreed on substantial tariff cuts that were phased in over the 1966–1972 period. Canada did not participate fully in the Kennedy Round, in part because of concerns about the competitiveness of Canada's manufacturing base, which was dominated by branch plants. Canada did, however, implement unilateral tariff reductions in the early 1970s. In the Tokyo Round, Canada engaged in a substantial reduction of trade barriers that was implemented in the 1980–1987 period. As a result, Canadian manufacturing industries faced, and accomplished, a major adjustment to trade liberalization.

Paradoxically, at the same time that Canada was pursuing more outward-looking trade policies, it was imposing more restrictive and nationalist investment policies. In the early 1970s, Canada created the Foreign Investment Review Agency and passed Bill C-58, which provided preferential tax treatment for advertisers in Canadian media. Again, in the early 1980s, there was a wave of nationalism in Canada associated with the second oil shock and the challenge of the sovereignty-association referendum in Quebec. The result was the National Energy Program (NEP), which was intended to promote greater Canadian ownership in the energy sector.

These two contradictory tendencies—more open trade policies and more nationalist investment policies—were confronted in the free trade negotiations with the United States. During Canada's free trade debate of 1987–1988, there was great concern about the perceived loss of Canadian sovereignty from participating in a Canada-U.S. Free Trade Agreement (CUFTA). More recently, the congressional debates about the North American Free Trade Agreement (NAFTA) in November 1993 and the implementation of the Uruguay Round and the World Trade Organization (WTO) in the autumn of 1994 have raised concerns about sovereignty in the United States.

Let us look back a decade to Canada's free trade debate in the mid-1980s.

Concerns about Free Trade: Ten Years After

Some of the Canadian concerns about free trade were identified a decade ago in a monograph prepared by Richard Lipsey and the author for the C.D. Howe Institute.[4]

Political Autonomy

One of Canada's main concerns was that close economic association with the United States would result in a political union between the two countries. In 1972, Mitchell Sharp, one of the best known of the modern exponents of this view, wrote that

> this option [a CUFTA] has been rejected in the past because it was judged to be inconsistent with Canada's desire to pre-

serve a maximum degree of independence, not because it lacked economic sense in terms of Canadian living standards and the stability of the Canadian economy.[5]

In 1984, he reiterated:

> To enter into a free trade arrangement with the United States is to alter fundamentally the direction of Canadian policy, not so much in economic terms as in political terms, and Canadians are not prepared to do so.[6]

But how valid are these concerns? It is useful to consider several examples.

The experience of the EC. On the one hand, the EC is very different from the CUFTA case because it contains several small as well as several large countries. On the other hand, being a common market rather than a free trade area, the EC represents a much closer arrangement than anything contemplated in CUFTA or NAFTA. Finally, and most interestingly, the early postwar fathers of the EC, such as Belgium's Spaak and France's Monnet, hoped that the logic of the emerging economic association would force closer political association and that this would end in something approximating a United States of Europe. Yet this political union, in spite of being wanted by the participants, has not come close to being achieved. There have been successive efforts—the Single European Act, the Single Market, and the Maastricht treaty—that have been pursued in an effort to achieve some measure of political union. The impression is created that political integration requires the continual mobilization of political will and is difficult to achieve.

Supporters of CUFTA argued that a much less comprehensive association than the EC—one that made much less drastic change in trade barriers and that was between two countries wishing to retain their independence—would not end up forcing on either partner a political association that it strongly opposed.

U.S. attitudes. So far, U.S. desires for political union with Canada have not been considered. The Canadian worry was that the United States was eagerly waiting to gobble up Canada politically. Somehow this view seems to be a bit naive in light of U.S. political institutions, practical U.S. politics—think of all those new seats in the Senate!—and the long, difficult struggle to bring into the union those two willing suppliants, Alaska and Hawaii.

Canadian political independence improved by CUFTA. Canada's dependence on U.S. markets indeed makes it quite vulnerable to U.S. policy shifts. CUFTA would formalize Canada's economic relationship with the United States in a way that would make it less liable to suffer from sudden, unilateral shifts in U.S. policy. This would reduce Canadian vulnerability and, therefore, increase the room for independent Canadian political maneuver.

Canadian political resilience. Those who doubt Canada's political resilience should study the case of the independence movement in Quebec. The United States fought a bloody civil war over the right of the southern states to secede. Spain, France, Yugoslavia, and a host of other countries seek to suppress the separatist movements of minorities, and, in the case of Yugoslavia, the result has been a bloody civil war. Canada is rare among nations in having allowed two referenda on separatism in which only the province considering secession voted! The rarity of this Canadian experience and the highly civilized nature of its conflict-resolution process are remarkable. There is always a risk that patience will wear thin and violence erupt with a third or fourth referendum (the never-endum), but so far the process has been remarkably civil.

Perceptions of the Outside World

Surely, would not the rest of the world believe that a free trade area would result in Canada being a U.S. political and economic satellite, and would not Canada lose influence as a result? This fear may be more realistic than the previous one. On the one hand, a Canadian government might wish to return to the halcyon days when Nobel Peace Prize winner Lester B. Pearson presented Canada's face abroad as honest broker. On the other hand, it might wish to come much closer to the kind of all-out support for U.S. foreign policy that is given, say, by the current U.K. government.

First, consider possible new constraints that a free trade agreement might put on Canadian political action. It would seem that any Canadian government has both of the above options open to it, and that these options can be exercised quite independently of the level of restrictions on Canada-U.S. trade.

On the contrary, CUFTA would prevent the United States from using commercial policy to express its disapproval of some Canadian political initiative—something it has done to other countries.

On this point consider the different approach of Canada and the United States to the question of trade and economic relations with Cuba. Canada (and Mexico as well) has persisted with trade relations and is likely to challenge some aspects of the Helms-Burton legislation under NAFTA.

Next, consider possible changes in Canada's external political image. This is a more subtle worry: if Canada lies down with the United States in a commercial bed, would it not lose credibility as an independent political force in the eyes of other countries? This worry is difficult to assess because it depends on opinion rather than fact. After all, there is a strong strain of anti-Americanism in many countries (and not just in contiguous countries).

Canada's perceived independence from U.S. foreign policy depends on the conduct of Canada's foreign policy. On the one hand, if Canada were to take strong and independent lines that sometimes risked U.S. disfavor, Canadian foreign policy would be perceived as being independent of the United States—even if bilateral tariff rates were zero. On the other hand, if Canada were to closely follow, and support, every twist and turn of U.S. foreign policy, it would be perceived as being a U.S. satellite, *even if bilateral tariff rates were very high.*

The italicized point is important. Few Canadians believe that high tariffs would save Canada from being thought a U.S. political satellite if the country acted like one. By the same token, low tariffs would not prevent Canada from being perceived as politically independent if it acted independently.

So far, only political issues have been discussed. No doubt third countries would correctly perceive that, with CUFTA, Canada would be even more closely linked economically to the United States. Possibly this would cause Canada to be more dependent on the United States in commercial policy. Were Canada to enter into a customs union, this would surely be true. The two countries would then have to harmonize their policies on trade restraints with third countries, and there would be little doubt which country's views would predominate in setting the common external policy.

But this did not happen with CUFTA or NAFTA. Canada continues to be free to operate its own independent policy on trade relations with the outside world. Canada and the United States pursued quite separate negotiation strategies during the Uruguay Round of GATT negotiations, and the Canadian government proceeded with free trade negotiations with Chile without the United States. So, on the question of the perception of third countries of Canadian independence, in the long term it depends on how much Canada exercises that independence in practice.

Social and Cultural Concerns

Some very difficult issues involving specific cultural support policies arise because of economic integration and the rapid pace of technological change in the information society.

Erosion of Canada's cultural independence. One concern is that a free trade agreement would erode Canada's cultural independence. The resonance of this concern depends on how one views the state of Canadian culture. There are those who seriously believe that there is no independent Canadian culture. For them, there is obviously no concern about erosion. The majority believes that although there are many similarities between Canadians and Americans based partly on their sharing similar national experiences—experiences that are very different from those of Europeans—there are also many significant cultural differences. Some believe that the characteristics that differentiate Canadian from U.S. culture are fragile. They worry, therefore, that these differences are subject to serious erosion as a result of minor changes in the behavior of ordinary Canadians; for example, reading more U.S. magazines or watching more U.S. television programs. Finally, there are those who believe that there is a separate and deeply rooted Canadian culture that would be difficult to erode.

The evidence gathered by such empirical sociologists as Seymour Martin Lipset suggests two key points.[7] First, Canadians and Americans are divided by some profound differences in attitudes on a host of matters ranging from such broad issues as global defense strategy, the welfare state, and respect for and trust in the police, down to such details as minor infractions of the law and identification with distinctive hero types in novels. Of course, there are differences among Americans and among Canadians, and one can find some Canadians who hold the typical U.S. attitude on any particular matter. But attitude surveys, as well as other evidence such as divorce rates, church attendance, and what is written in novels, show the typical Canadian attitude on issue after issue to be significantly different from that of the typical American.

The second point is that there are plausible reasons for believing that these attitudinal differences are deeply rooted and, hence, will be resilient to such culturally homogenizing forces as reading the same magazines and watching the same movies and television shows. The reasons for these documented cultural differences will always be open to debate but, as explained by Lipset, some of them surely lie in our very different heritages. There is space to mention only two illustrations here.

First, consider the way in which each country achieved political independence. The United States has a revolutionary background. During the American Revolution, however, Canada received the Loyalists, who rejected the revolution and instead chose allegiance to the British Crown. *Les canadiens* were also conservative in their values and outlook and did not live through the cathartic rejection of the church during the French Revolution. Reflecting these social characteristics, Canada's political independence was the result of a process of devolution, not revolution.

Second, consider the timing of foreign immigration. Massive immigration changed the face of U.S. society in the nineteenth century. Until well after World War II, however, the Canadian population—although not, of course, every Canadian area—was dominated by people whose forebears came from France or the British Isles. Then, in the postwar world, under a very different social climate from that which greeted nineteenth-century immigrants to the United States, Canada opened its doors and became a genuinely multiracial society.

Private and public support for cultural activities. Here the concern is that CUFTA would reduce, or destroy, some of the private markets and eliminate some of the public policies that support many of Canada's cultural activities. Canadian government support for broadly defined cultural activities is substantial for three primary reasons:

- although the product can be sold on the market, the local market is not large enough to support the activity—at least with the degree of diversity policymakers think desirable;

- the market is large enough, but the share that would go to Canadian producers in open competition with U.S. producers is not great enough to support them; and

- an objective of public policy is to produce a product different from one that would emerge if the product had to be sustained by free-market activity.

The first case involves subsidies to support a host of up-market cultural activities such as theaters, art galleries, museums, and orchestras. CUFTA would create no problem with respect to any of these activities. They are subsidized in many countries, and there is nothing in the conditions of a typical free trade agreement that would interfere with such support.

The third case is typified by the Canadian Broadcasting Corporation. Its product would be very different if its revenues depended only on advertising and other commercially determined sources. The main challenge here is to find the revenues to support this kind of activity at a time of high government debt service costs.

Problems arise with the second case. Here, the market is large enough to sustain some activity—say, the publishing of several weekly news magazines. But given the share of the market that U.S. magazines would obtain in open competition, the volume of sales available to Canadian magazines would be below the minimum needed to sustain some of the Canadian publications. The same argument applies to television stations. There is room for one or more stations in an area, but given the volume of advertising that Canadian firms would place with U.S. stations, there would not be enough advertising revenue to sustain some of the existing Canadian stations.

Canadian support policy could then take one of two basic forms. Either some method could be found to transfer to Canadian firms the revenues that would otherwise be earned by U.S. firms, or a subsidy—either direct or indirect—could be given to allow Canadian firms to survive with the sales that they can make in open competition with U.S. firms.

Whatever the reasons, Canadian support policy has often provided direct restrictions on foreign competition instead of subsidies to Canadian producers. Consider a few of the most important of these: Canadian newspapers, periodicals, books, recordings, radio stations, films, and television broadcasters receive substantial support. Federal sales taxes are remitted;

importation of foreign periodicals with more than 5 percent of their advertising expressly aimed at Canada is prohibited; direct financial assistance goes to Canadian publishers; there is much provincial support of Canadian-owned publishers; and there is substantial, but varying, support of the film and television industries.

Bill C-58.   Under Bill C-58, which has applied for more than 20 years, Canada-based companies are not allowed to deduct advertising expenses incurred with non-Canadian media for advertising aimed at Canadian audiences. This applies to print media—newspapers and periodicals—and to television and radio broadcasters. Qualifying as "Canadian" requires satisfying both Canadian-ownership and Canadian-content requirements.

When this bill was first passed in the 1970s, it caused a furor south of the border. The law is probably inconsistent with any concept of free trade in services because it puts U.S. media at a serious disadvantage in competing with Canadian media for Canadian advertising dollars. Assuming that Canadian border stations could not stand up to open competition with U.S. border stations for advertisers' dollars—about which, more below—and assuming that Canadian magazines could not stand up to competition from Canadian editions of such U.S. magazines as *Time*, we may then ask whether there are other policies that would allow these Canadian media to survive but that would not come into conflict with the conditions of a typical free trade area.

Tax incentives versus subsidies.   In principle, most things that can be done with tax incentives or with quantity restrictions can also be done with direct subsidies. There is little doubt, for example, that those Canadian border stations, magazines, and periodicals that could not otherwise cover costs could be kept in business with an appropriate government subsidy. Furthermore, such a subsidy would be less likely to encounter U.S. opposition than did Bill C-58. The U.S. government has never suggested that it would object to direct Canadian subsidies for this purpose. Such subsidies would not, for example, stop U.S. border stations competing for Canadian advertising dollars on open terms with Canadian stations. Such subsidies could be lump-sum grants, or they could be given on a per-unit basis related to readership or listening audience, thus rewarding success. In principle, they could also be given through the placement of sufficient government advertising to increase revenues to a viable amount.

A rational view of policy suggests some advantage to using the subsidy approach. It is open and its cost could, therefore, be readily calculated. It would allow users to choose freely among competing U.S. and Canadian products. If consumers showed very little interest in the Canadian product, government support might be reconsidered; if the Canadian product showed itself able to maintain a significant part of the market, the subsidy would more likely be regarded as worthwhile.

Other methods of subsidization could no doubt be invented. The problem with any subsidy plan, however, is in its political acceptability. Special-interest groups prefer direct restrictions on the ability of U.S. producers to compete because restrictions have concealed costs that are not easy to calculate and, therefore, are less likely to arouse public objection. Also, restrictions might protect the Canadian product from serious competition and, thus, allow it to sustain itself even if it became inferior to the foreign product on all counts.

Furthermore, governments do not like direct subsidies because they place the cost within the government's budget, while regulatory methods place the cost on the private sector. Special-interest groups do not like subsidies because, by making the degree of subsidization obvious and the payments subject to government review, the net effect is often less support than when the cost is hidden and diffused throughout the private sector.[8]

Although these issues were debated at the time of the free trade negotiations, the Canadian government chose to avoid the issue by exempting culture from both CUFTA and NAFTA. The U.S. quid pro quo for this exception was a right of retaliation.

The border broadcasting case—an illustration. The key assumption in the advertising tax case is that intervention is needed to preserve the financial viability of many border radio and television stations. An internal government study paper, however, casts some doubt on this premise. After a careful study of the facts, the paper concludes that the increase in total revenues of all border television stations due to Bill C-58 was $30 million, which, according to the paper, is about 4 percent of the total revenues of all the affected stations.[9] Furthermore, the U.S. border stations expressed a willingness to pay Canadian taxes by setting up Canadian subsidiaries and prorating their revenues so that revenue from Canadian sources would be taxed in

Canada.[10] Thus, it becomes doubtful that the principal effect of the policy was to support stations that would otherwise have failed. Different consequences, which have been so often found in other cases of government regulatory behavior, suggest themselves.

Economic Concerns

While sophisticated observers (such as Mitchell Sharp quoted above) were more concerned about the political and cultural effects of free trade, some Canadians worried about the economic impact. They were worried that Canadians would become merely hewers of wood and drawers of water, that the much-maligned multinationals would withdraw from Canada, and that the Canadian economy would simply deindustrialize. Some of these critics, having predicted dire consequences from free trade, concluded that all job losses in Canada's 1990–1991 recession were due to the impact of CUFTA.[11]

Before examining these extreme economic concerns more closely, let us examine the more subtle concerns about the economic pressures to harmonize a wide range of domestic policies.

Harmonization effects. Harmonization effects arise as a result of market pressures or through response to implicit or explicit threats of unilateral actions. In general, harmonization pressures arise because of differences in the relative price of goods or factors. Such pressures can occur through legal channels (for example, democratic societies rarely impose emigration controls on highly educated workers) or through illegal channels (tobacco smuggling, for example).

A simple general theorem is an open economy extension of the optimal tax literature: the state ought to tax immobile factors and tastes. A corollary—the biblical injunction that the poor are always with us—is ever more valid because the highly skilled and highly educated are more mobile internationally. Moreover, what is regarded as immobile, for example, taxing tobacco consumption, may change in an open economy context. The tastes may be relatively immobile, at least in the short run, but the cigarettes are easily transported through illegal channels.

The nature of the policy intervention or measure influences the nature of the harmonization pressure. For example, agricultural price supports are extremely vulnerable to commodity arbitrage pressures if quantitative restrictions are removed from international trade. Highly skilled individuals, especially at certain stages of their careers, are affected more by high marginal tax rates than by public benefits. Similarly, investment decisions are significantly influenced by comparative corporate tax regimes.

This discussion focuses on harmonization pressures associated with relative prices for goods and services or relative factor returns. Another type of harmonization pressure arises from high mobility of short-term capital flows. When short-term financial assets are highly substitutable with comparable international assets, there will be a tight relationship between interest rate differentials and the forward premium (discount) on the exchange rate resulting from interest arbitrage. One consequence is that the real exchange rate, rather than real interest rates, becomes the major channel through which monetary policy operates. In this context, the effectiveness of Keynesian-type fiscal policies is reduced because in the normal case—say the United States in the early 1980s—the effect of a rising budget deficit puts upward pressure on domestic interest rates and leads to exchange rate appreciation. Thus, the induced capital flow is effected through a deterioration of the trade and current account balance, which offsets fairly quickly the effects of fiscal stimulus on aggregate demand. This line of analysis follows the Mundell-Fleming-Dornbusch analysis of small open economies.[12] Thus, in a very open economy, "crowding out" from budget deficits occurs through the current account instead of through reduced private sector investment as would be the case in a more closed economy.

The increasing integration and growing liquidity of global financial markets, and the proliferation of new financial instruments, have spawned concerns that the sovereignty of governments is held hostage by 22-year-old futures traders wearing suspenders and playing Nintendo on their computer screens. In fact, Canada has conducted macroeconomic policy within a context of highly liquid, highly substitutable capital flows since the 1950s. Indeed, it was the Canadian case that stimulated the early Mundell-Fleming analysis of small open economies with high mobility of short-term capital flows.

Modern global financial markets can be tolerant of macroeconomic policy independence, but periods of indulgence by the markets can be followed by overreaction in asset markets. The combination of large portfolio capital inflows into Mexico in the

1990–1994 period in anticipation of the benefits of NAFTA and the unsustainable macroeconomic policies in Mexico associated with the political cycle in the 1993–1994 period led to a sharp reaction in financial markets: the so-called peso crisis of late 1994 and early 1995.[13]

Another form of harmonization pressure operates through the threat of unilateral actions of trading partners in response to domestic policies. For example, the United States imposes countervailing duties against foreign subsidy practices and has threatened action under Section 301 because foreign countries had inadequate intellectual property protection or pursued other practices regarded as unfair. In recent years some in the United States and Europe have called for the use of trade sanctions to enforce foreign compliance with environmental, labor, or other regulatory standards in the home country.

Subsidies and the trade laws. From the U.S. perspective, U.S. import legislation provides a transparent, nonpolitical system for dealing with trade disputes that involve allegations of unfair trade and import disruptions caused by products acknowledged to be fairly traded. To Canadian exporters, however, the U.S. system seems to provide opportunities for competing interests in the United States to harass Canadian firms by subjecting them to the cost of defending expensive legal proceedings as well as to the risk of contending with apparently arbitrary trade barriers being imposed on Canadian products. Canadians felt that the decision by the U.S. International Trade Administration (ITA) to reverse its 1983 ruling on softwood lumber (which found Canadian stumpage policies—fees charged for the sale of timber—not to be countervailable subsidies under U.S. law) undermined the credibility of the claim that the U.S. system is nonpolitical.

Although the two countries have quite similar import regulation systems, asymmetries in trade and production between them mean that Canada has a greater interest in restricting application of import relief legislation than does the United States. In the smaller Canadian economy exports frequently account for a relatively larger share of production, and most of those exports go to the United States. Thus, the risk of U.S. import restrictions or duties significantly increases the risk to investment in new production facilities in Canada. The same cannot be said of the United States. Although plants located in

U.S. border states may send a high proportion of their output to Canada, it is relatively easy for them to shift sales to other parts of the United States if Canada imposes import duties.

Canada's dependence on exports to the United States can create problems from a U.S. perspective as well. A 1972 statement by the Canadian-American Committee presciently observed:

> Given the high percentage of Canadian production exported to the United States, Canadian policies to head off unemployment through subsidizing production might often appear in American eyes to be export subsidies, and be answered as such.[14]

The potential application of U.S. countervailing duties is a particular source of concern to Canadians because the threat of such duties impinges on Canada's choice of domestic economic policies. This was first illustrated by the 1973 Michelin tire decision, in which the United States found Canadian regional development subsidies to be a countervailable subsidy. Before that decision, the U.S. Treasury had applied countervailing duties only to more specific cases of explicit export subsidies. After the Trade Agreement Act of 1979, which implemented the Tokyo Round subsidies code, countervailing duties could be imposed on any domestic subsidies that are specific or not widely available. Decisions by the U.S. Court of International Trade in the mid-1980s, however, cast some doubt on this interpretation.[15]

These court decisions, and a subsequent administrative review by the ITA, were factors in the 1986 decision by a U.S. producer group—the Coalition for Fair Lumber Imports—to resubmit a petition seeking countervailing duties on softwood lumber.

The Gibbons bill, introduced in 1985 and incorporated into the omnibus trade bill of 1986, represented a legislative effort to broaden further the definition of subsidy in U.S. countervailing duty law in a manner that was aimed at Canadian resource policies. This provision was intended to overturn the ITA's 1983 softwood products decision. Congressional action was preempted by the U.S. Commerce Department's October 1986 preliminary ruling that Canadian stumpage policies constituted a subsidy. Canadians saw this ruling as an encroachment on their economic and political sovereignty. In their view, an agency of the U.S. government was passing judgment on the long-standing resource tenure systems and stumpage practices of the Canadian provinces by declaring them to constitute unfair trade. Thus, the trend toward a broadening of the U.S. definition of what constitutes a countervailable subsidy operates as an increasing constraint on the domestic policies of Canadian governments.

Canada finds itself in a uniquely difficult position on subsidies and countervailing duties. More than any other country, Canada is vulnerable to the imposition of U.S. countervailing duties directed against foreign subsidies. The subsidy wars that occurred between the EC and the United States on agriculture during the 1980s provide a typical case in which Canada has been caught in the crossfire because there was no effective mechanism to control subsidies that increase exports to third-country markets.

Canada and the United States found it impossible to negotiate rules for subsidies and countervailing duties or antidumping duties in the CUFTA negotiations. After 1988 these issues were transferred to the multilateral forum of the Uruguay Round, and there was no negotiation of these issues in NAFTA.

Where Are We Now?

It is difficult to assess all the effects of CUFTA and NAFTA in a short paper, but some summary observations are possible. The more extreme economic concerns about free trade can be reflected. None of the critics of CUFTA and NAFTA, who advanced the extreme view that every job lost in 1990 and 1991 was due to CUFTA, have repeated these claims about NAFTA because during the 1993–1995 period the Canadian economy experienced a sustained recovery with significant expansion in total employment. Of course, there are grounds for criticism of the precise timing of Canada's disinflation policy and the mix of monetary and fiscal policy, which contributed to the severity of the 1990–1991 recession.[16]

Thus, for the purposes of this paper, let us examine the longer-term shift in the pattern of trade and economic structure that has occurred over the last decade, as CUFTA and NAFTA have been implemented in the context of the longer-term trend to increased trade between Canada and the United States.

Differences in Economic Structure

If we look back to the 1950s, the division of labor between Canada and the United States was a vertical division, with Canada dependent on the export of unprocessed or semiprocessed resource commodities and with a protected manufacturing sector oriented to import substitution. In 1960, for example, more than 90 percent of Canadian exports were primary or semiprocessed resource commodities. This structure tended to lead to manic-depressive mood swings in the economic relationship, with Canadian nationalism rising because of rising resource prices during economic booms and the United States becoming protectionist during recessions. Canada enacted nationalist investment regulations in 1972, 1973, and 1980, when commodity prices were booming, while the United States enacted protectionist measures in 1970–1971 and 1982–1983 in the aftermath of serious recessions. For example, in the 1982–1983 period the first countervailing duty case was brought against Canadian exports of lumber. The case was rejected, however, when the U.S. Department of Commerce ruled that the Canadian stumpage practices were not countervailable under U.S. law.

Tables 1 & 2 demonstrate the significant expansion of trade between Canada and the United States during the 1988–1993 period. The 1990–1992 recession affected the year-to-year growth rate of trade, but over the five-year period there was a strong increase in bilateral trade. Although many in Canada had been concerned that CUFTA would lead to a deindustrialization of the economy and a reversion by Canada to exporting natural resources, the share of manufactured products in Canada's exports increased from 1988 to 1993, with the most rapid growth in nonautomotive manufactured products.

CUFTA appears to have benefited both countries in stimulating trade and economic growth amidst the prolonged recession of the early 1990s. Many enterprises, both large and small, in both countries have responded to the competitive challenges and opportunities resulting from the removal of trade barriers between Canada and the United States.

Apart from the debate about the shorter-term impact of CUFTA and NAFTA, the longer-term impact of the two trade agreements appears to be consolidating the postwar trend of greater economic integration between Canada and the United States. This has led to a more horizontal division of labor with intraindustry specialization within manufacturing and services replacing the interindustry specialization of Canada exporting resources and importing manufactures.

Over time the shift to a more horizontal pattern of specialization between the Canadian and U.S. economies should moderate the potential for bilateral trade and investment disputes.

There was significant unfinished business under CUFTA and NAFTA, however, in the form of outstanding issues that were left for future resolution.

When the Liberal government came to power in October 1993, it had some reservations about NAFTA, which had been negotiated but not yet implemented. Before agreeing to proceed with NAFTA, the Canadian government obtained letters from the U.S. government confirming that Canada had not jeopardized its water resources by entering into NAFTA and obtained a commitment to set up working groups to develop a substitute regime for the antidumping and countervailing duty laws.

The NAFTA Working Groups

The three NAFTA governments established working groups to deal with the unfinished trade rules under NAFTA. These issues include the development of rules for subsidies and countervailing duties, the application of antidumping duty laws, and the effectiveness of dispute settlement mechanisms within NAFTA.

The subsidies and countervailing duty arrangements resulting from the Uruguay Round and incorporated in the WTO appear to provide a very useful basis for dealing with these issues in a North American context. In particular, the subsidies agreement (and also the agriculture agreement) under the WTO do impose some limits or disciplines on the use of subsidies in the three NAFTA partners. The question remains, however, whether Canada, the United States, and Mexico are prepared to contemplate greater discipline in the use of subsidies within the North American context, which would allow the three countries to go further in reducing the application of countervailing duties within the North American market.

The arrangements with respect to antidumping laws under the WTO will have only modest impact on the application of these laws within North America. There is a strong economic case for reform of the antidumping laws in NAFTA as the integration process proceeds, but there is no consensus about how these trade rules ought to evolve. The reduction or culmination of other trade barriers within NAFTA is already leading to greater integration of production and trade. What are the consequences of this integration process for the economic effects of the antidumping laws within NAFTA? As NAFTA integration proceeds, what are the implications for the business strategies of firms in the North American marketplace?

Table 1
Canadian Domestic Exports

	1988	1989	1990	1991	1992	1993
To the World (millions of Can$)						
Total	138,498	138,701	148,979	145,887	162,823	187,348
Agriculture	11,726	10,002	11,589	12,045	14,126	13,790
Raw materials	17,444	18,349	19,586	19,057	20,347	21,657
Semiprocessed products	48,356	48,008	47,573	45,800	50,101	56,928
Automotiveproducts	34,494	33,755	34,325	32,527	37,844	47,462
Other manufactured products	22,143	24,018	27,034	27,378	30,277	35,580
Special transactions	691	711	1,614	1,686	1,751	2,037
To the United States (millions of Can$)						
Total	100,851	101,592	111,557	109,614	125,670	150,542
Agriculture	4,344	4,389	5,175	5,440	6,666	7,951
Raw materials	9,182	9,787	11,242	11,627	13,726	15,225
Semiprocessed products	33,421	32,463	33,091	31,731	35,802	43,078
Automotive products	33,870	33,158	33,775	31,918	37,074	46,496
Other manufactured products	16,665	18,329	20,719	21,317	23,854	27,812
Special transactions	578	576	1,451	1,428	1,543	1,832

Table 1, continued
Canadian Domestic Exports

	1988	1989	1990	1991	1992	1993
To the United States (percentage share of total)						
Total	72.82	73.25	74.88	75.14	77.18	80.35
Agriculture	3.14	3.16	3.47	3.73	4.09	4.24
Raw materials	6.63	7.06	7.55	7.97	8.43	8.13
Semiprocessed products	24.13	23.41	22.21	21.75	21.99	22.99
Automotive products	24.46	23.91	22.67	21.88	22.77	24.82
Other manufactured products	12.03	13.21	13.91	14.61	14.65	14.85
Special transactions	0.42	0.42	0.97	0.98	0.95	0.98
To the United States (percentage growth rate)						
Total		0.73	9.81	-1.74	14.65	19.79
Agriculture		1.04	17.91	5.12	22.54	19.28
Raw materials		6.59	14.87	3.42	18.05	10.92
Semiprocessed products		-2.87	1.93	-4.11	12.83	20.32
Automotive products		-2.10	1.86	-5.50	16.15	25.41
Other manufactured products		9.98	13.04	2.89	11.90	16.59
Special transactions		-0.35	151.91	-1.59	8.05	18.73

Source: CANSIM, Statistics Canada, Ottawa, June 1994

Table 2
Canadian Imports

	1988	1989	1990	1991	1992	1993
From the World (millions of Can$)						
Total	131,172	135,191	136,224	135,454	148,013	169,951
Agriculture	13,992	15,352	17,262	16,235	17,122	19,073
Raw materials	6,970	7,854	9,273	7,965	8,145	8,975
Semiprocessed products	89,240	90,452	89,358	90,625	99,483	114,479
Automotive products	33,617	32,127	30,618	31,125	33,867	40,052
Other manufactured products	27,527	29,291	29,484	28,159	32,346	38,618
Special transactions	2,670	2,884	2,963	3,634	4,061	4,350
From the United States (millions of Can$)						
Total	86,021	88,103	87,895	86,406	96,468	113,044
Agriculture	6,870	7,328	7,414	7,330	8,216	9,395
Raw materials	3,249	3,392	3,112	2,724	3,012	3,445
Semiprocessed products	16,210	17,564	18,544	17,521	19,546	23,008
Automotive products	27,506	25,833	23,702	23,078	25,832	32,181
Other manufactured products	33,640	35,585	36,400	36,205	40,381	46,488
Special transactions	1,687	1,673	1,738	2,123	2,355	2,604

Table 2, continued
Canadian Imports

	1988	1989	1990	1991	1992	1993
From the United States (percentage share of total)						
Total	65.58	65.17	64.52	63.79	65.18	66.52
Agriculture	5.24	5.42	5.44	5.41	5.55	5.53
Raw materials	2.48	2.51	2.28	2.01	2.03	2.03
Semi-processed products	12.36	12.99	13.61	12.94	13.21	13.54
Automotive products	20.97	19.11	17.40	17.04	17.45	18.94
Other manufactured products	25.65	26.32	26.72	26.73	27.28	27.35
Special transac tions	1.29	1.24	1.28	1.57	1.59	1.53
From the United States (percentage growth rate)						
Total		2.42	-0.24	-1.69	11.65	17.18
Agriculture		6.67	1.17	-1.13	12.09	14.35
Raw materials		4.40	-8.25	-12.47	10.57	14.38
Semiprocessed products		8.35	5.58	-5.52	11.56	17.71
Automotive products		-6.08	-8.25	-2.63	11.93	24.58
Other manufactured products		5.78	2.29	-0.54	11.53	15.12
Special transactions		-0.83	3.89	22.15	10.93	10.57

Source: CANSIM, Statistics Canada, Ottawa, June 1994

Whatever the economic logic for the reform of the anti-dumping laws as the removal of other trade barriers proceeds, the political economy of these issues has not changed sufficiently as yet. The NAFTA working groups were unable to achieve any substantive changes within their two-year mandate.

Cultural Issues and the Information Highway

The cultural exemption has not been a major issue until recently, but disputes have arisen recently and longer-term challenges arise from the impact of technological change. In late 1994, Canada invoked provisions under the Canadian Radio-Television and Telecommunications Commission licensing procedures to remove the license of a country music channel originating from the United States because a Canadian company applied for a license. Also in December 1994, Canada imposed special taxes on the sale of the U.S. magazine *Sports Illustrated* in Canada because, although the magazine was printed in Canada, it contained editorial layout transmitted electronically from the United States.[17] Although the broad cultural exemption under NAFTA that was carried forward from CUFTA means that Canada arguably is not breaking international obligations, by the same provisions the United States has wide latitude to enact countermeasures. Some of the Canadian measures, however, could be challenged under the provisions of GATT and the WTO.

Although it is doubtful that the broad cultural exemption is useful under NAFTA, the presence of the provision in CUFTA and NAFTA reflects political sensitivity in Canada to perceived cultural domination by the dynamic U.S. entertainment and media industries. Canada remains reluctant to negotiate rules for trade and investment in the cultural area, but the pressure of technological change and the fusion of the telecommunications, computer, and broadcast industries are likely to make this policy increasingly difficult to sustain.

Agriculture

It is unfortunate that an overall trade balance within a sector is not sufficient to assure harmonious trade relations. The U.S. Department of Commerce indicated that the United States exported $5.9 billion to Canada and imported $5.6 billion in food, feeds, and beverages in 1993, yet the agrifood sector is a source of serious frictions between the two countries.

Bilateral agricultural issues have proved very difficult to resolve, and during 1994 the United States threatened to take action under NAFTA attacking the new high tariffs that Canada is imposing to replace the quotas on imports of dairy products and poultry as a result of the Uruguay Round agriculture agreement. At the same time, the United States sought to impose restrictions on the export of Canadian wheat to the United States; it based its initiative on an interpretation of the Uruguay Round agreements that used an argument for wheat restrictions similar to one Canada used to defend high tariffs on imports of supply-managed commodities.

Yet how did we get here? Part of the purpose of CUFTA, NAFTA, and the Uruguay Round was to create a better framework for resolving these sorts of issues. In CUFTA the two countries agreed to remove tariffs and some nontariff barriers on bilateral agricultural trade as well as remove export subsidies from bilateral shipments. The tough issues, however—quota restrictions on sugar, dairy, and peanuts in the United States and on dairy and poultry in Canada, domestic farm subsidies, and agricultural export subsidies in third markets—were put aside to be dealt with in the Uruguay Round.

Unfortunately, the Uruguay Round was delayed and implementation did not start until 1995. In the meantime, bilateral frictions festered. Export subsidies such as the U.S. export enhancement program will be reduced but not eliminated by 2002. Reflecting concerns of dairy farmers who are concentrated in Quebec and of poultry farmers, Canada has converted import quotas into high tariffs under the agriculture chapter of the WTO. The United States is imposing tough restrictions on sugar-containing and peanut products from Canada and is seeking significant tariffs on wheat from Canada. At the same time, the United States is challenging the Canadian tariff rate quotas for dairy products.

Some U.S. farm groups perceive that Canada obtains lopsided benefits from CUFTA's agricultural chapter, which is continued under NAFTA. Although the overall levels of subsidies in the key commodity groups in the two countries may be similar and in some cases Canadian subsidies are much lower, differences in the farm programs, administrative arrangements, and delivery mechanisms are sources of perceptions of unfairness.

The Uruguay Round rules for agricultural subsidies are an important step, but only a step, toward resolution of these problems.

The sovereignty issue for Canada in agriculture is primarily a concern about maintaining very protectionist dairy policies in response to the political pressure of the sovereignty movement in Quebec.

The Quebec Question

The internal stresses within the Canadian federation with the election of a Parti Quebecois government and the aftermath of the referendum will influence the dynamic of the Canada-U.S. relationship. The very narrow victory of the federalists in the Quebec referendum of October 1995 suggests that the sovereignty issue will be contested again in the next few years. An eventual sovereignty scenario would be divisive within Canada, and even after the serious economic dislocation of the adjustment process, both Quebec and the rest of Canada will be weakened in their dealings with the United States.

Acute challenges for Canada-U.S. economic relations could arise if Quebec were to declare its sovereignty and secede from the Canadian federation. There would also be intense political and security challenges. The aboriginal peoples in northern Quebec and some parts of Quebec with substantial Anglophone populations might wish, in turn, to secede from Quebec.

Even if Canada and Quebec could resolve the difficult questions surrounding debt and boundaries and could agree to maintain some form of a free trade agreement permitting relatively free movement of goods and services between these two economies, there would still be complex issues in managing economic relations with major economic partners and in dealing with the very fluid and volatile international negotiating agenda.

One of the economic gains from the present federation in Canada that is often overlooked is the conduct of trade diplomacy.[18] Whether it is dealing with trade disputes under the former CUFTA, NAFTA, or GATT or WTO or dealing with international economic negotiations, the economic size and viability of the Canadian Customs Union influence Canada's international economic leverage. With respect to trade disputes, the ultimate enforcement mechanism under GATT or CUFTA is the threat of trade retaliation. Trade retaliation is seldom invoked under GATT and was never invoked under CUFTA, yet the potential threat of such retaliation does influence the bargaining position of parties to a trade dispute in the negotiations that inevitably follow adjudication by GATT-WTO panels or CUFTA/NAFTA panels under the Chapter 18/20 dispute settlement process. It is evident in GATT-WTO and NAFTA that an economy such as Canada's has rather more bargaining leverage for the settlement of trade disputes than does a small economy like Nicaragua's, which had a trade dispute with the United States under GATT.

A Quebec sovereignty scenario would create a crisis in bilateral relations without precedent in this century. The dynamics between the U.S. Congress and the U.S. administration will influence and likely complicate the Canada-U.S.-Quebec dynamic. As evidence on this point, consider the negative reaction of the Congress to the Clinton administration's proposed loan package for Mexico to help it over the liquidity crisis following the peso devaluation. Despite support from the Republican leadership, a coalition of anti-NAFTA Democrats and populist Republicans was able to block the proposal despite the direct interests of U.S. jobs tied to exports to Mexico and the interests of the U.S. financial community in restoring confidence in the markets.

The key longer-term problem is that NAFTA and WTO provide a much weaker institutional and political framework for economic integration than does the European Union. Indeed the NAFTA framework is weaker than was the EC prior to the Single European Act.

This creates two problems. First, the Canadian economic union could unravel to the much lower level of integration of NAFTA. The viability of the currency union and the customs union would be in doubt. Second, because Canada relies on international trade agreements and dispute settlement procedures to manage the bilateral relationship, the effectiveness of these processes is conditioned by the size of the economies involved because the ultimate sanction is the threat of trade retaliation.

Even if the sovereignty scenario is rejected yet again in a future referendum, in the meantime Canadian sensitivity over national unity concerns may harden Canadian positions on issues such as protection of the dairy sector or the cultural industries, making it more difficult to resolve these issues in bilateral negotiations with the United States. Many observers have noted the prominent role of Quebec in supporting the negotiation and implementation of CUFTA, but less widely noted is that the sovereignty debate of 1980 intensified the economic nationalism of the last Trudeau government as manifest in the NEP, which was a source of friction in the Canada-U.S. relationship. The question is whether the enduring challenge of Quebec's relations with the rest of Canada will be a major source of stress in the Canada-U.S. relationship.

Conclusion

The economic integration under CUFTA and NAFTA seems to be consolidating a more horizontal division of labor and a more symmetric pattern of investment between the two economies, which over the longer term should moderate some mood swings in the relationship. Economic nationalism seems to be moderating in Canada, and the economic integration under NAFTA seems to be reinforcing that trend. Old problems such as agricultural subsidies and trade barriers and rules for antidumping and countervailing duties remain largely unresolved, however, and new stresses are emerging over the future of cultural protection by Canada while death stars and the information highway are undermining the use of regulated monopolies as instruments of state policy.

The continuing debate over Quebec sovereignty will persist in influencing the political context and could harden Canadian positions on issues ranging from protection of Quebec dairy farmers to the protective measures for cultural industries. A Quebec sovereignty scenario could produce a serious crisis in Canada-U.S. relations.

The overall conclusion that can be drawn is that although economic integration is occurring between Canada and the United States as trade barriers are removed, this economic integration is not leading down a slippery slope of surrender of sovereignty by Canadian governments. Unlike in Europe, where there have been repeated efforts to deepen economic integration and to foster political integration, there seems little political will in the three NAFTA countries to deepen economic integration, let alone to foster political integration.

Notes

1. Canada and the United States did dispute the right of passage for oil tankers through the High Arctic islands, but this was a diplomatic dispute without recourse to gunboats.

2. J.H. Young, *Canadian Commercial Policy*, study prepared for Royal Commission on Canada's Economic Prospects (Ottawa: Queen's Printer, 1957), 30.

3. Ibid.

4. Richard Lipsey and Murray G. Smith, *Taking the Initiative: Canada's Trade Options in a Turbulent World* (Toronto: C. D. Howe Institute, 1985).

5. Mitchell Sharp, "Canada-U.S. Relations: Options for the Future," *International Perspectives—Special Issue* (Ottawa: External Affairs Canada, Autumn 1972), 15.

6. M. Sharp, "Canada's Independence and U.S. Domination," in *U.S.-Canadian Economic Relations: Next Steps?* ed. E. R. Fried and P. H. Trezise (Washington, D.C.: The Brookings Institution, 1984), 17.

7. R.G. Lipsey, "Canada and the United States: The Economic Dimension," and S. M. Lipset, "Canada and the United States: The Cultural Dimension," both in *Canada and the United States: Enduring Friendship, Persistent Stress*, ed. C. F. Doran and J. H. Sigler (New York: Prentice-Hall, 1985). A more extensive treatment is S. M. Lipset, *Continental Divide: The Values and Institutions of the United States and Canada* (Washington, D.C.: Canadian-American Committee, 1989).

8. The enormous technological changes that are going on in the communications field will have serious ramifications for any support policy that is followed by the Canadian government. Commentators analyzing cultural policies have stressed the significance of the rapid pace of technological change that is occurring in the electronic media as a result of satellite transmission and the diffusion of video cassettes (see S. Globerman and A. Vining, "Bilateral Cultural Free Trade: The U.S.-Canadian Case" (Simon Fraser University, Vancouver, 1984, mimeographed). On the one hand, new technology is steadily reducing the distribution cost of certain types of cultural services such as television, sports, and video cassettes; thus, freer trade could result in even greater saturation of Canadian electronic media by U.S. content. On the other hand, these same shifts in technology are lowering the costs of reaching specialized audiences; hence, independent Canadian producers will face lower cost barriers to reaching those special segments of the more fragmented markets in both countries. Regardless of the net effects of technological change on the level of production of Canadian cultural industries, these trends to fragmentation and specialization are likely to render the existing set of trade restrictions obsolete. Given the rapid pace of technological change, subsidy policies are likely to be more robust in achieving the desired production levels than are quota restrictions.

9. A. Donner and M. Kliman, *Television Advertising and the Income Tax Act: An Economic Analysis of Bill C-58*, Draft Report (Ottawa: Department of Communications, November 1983).

10. D. Leyton-Brown, *Weathering the Storm: Canadian-U.S. Relations, 1980–83*, CAC No. 51 (Toronto; Washington, D.C.: Canadian-American Committee, 1985).

11. See Maude Barlow, *Parcel of Rogues: How Free Trade is Failing Canada* (Toronto: Key Porter Books, 1990) and Mel Hurtig, *The Betrayal of Canada* (Toronto: Stoddart, 1991).

12. See Richard G. Lipsey and Murray G. Smith, *Global Imbalances and U.S. Policy Responses* (Washington, D.C.: Canadian-American Committee, 1987).

13. See John Williamson, "Reform of the International Financial Institutions," *Canadian Foreign Policy* 3, no. 1 (1995): 15–22. Williamson discusses the Mexican "peso crisis" in the context of proposals for international financial institution (IFI) reform.

14. Canadian-American Committee, *The New Environment for Canadian-American Relations* (Washington, D.C.; Montreal: Canadian-American Committee, 1972), 34.

15. See *Bethlehem Steel Corp. v. United States and Highveld Steel and Vanadium Corp*, U.S. Court of International Trade (1984); and *Cabot Corp. v. United States*, U.S. Court of International Trade (1985).

16. See Thomas J. Courchene, "Canada in the 1990s: Coping with Internal and External Economic Change," in *Canadian Federalism: Meeting Global Economic Challenges?* ed. Douglas Brown and Murray Smith (Kingston and Halifax: Institute for Intergovernmental Relations and Institute for Research on Public Policy, 1991), 43–52.

17. Canadian customs regulations preventing split press runs for magazines had been maintained under CUFTA and NAFTA, but the possibility of electronic communication of the editorial content had not arisen previously.

18. These issues are discussed in *Canadian Federalism*, ed. Douglas Brown and Murray Smith; in Fanny S. Demers and Michel Demers, *The European Union: A Viable Model for Quebec-Canada?* (Ottawa: Centre for Trade Policy and Law, 1995); and in Charles E. Roh, Jr., *The Implications for U.S. Trade Policy of an Independent Quebec*, Policy Papers on the Americas (Washington, D.C.: Center for Strategic and International Studies and Centre for Trade Policy and Law, 1995).

3

Sovereignty: Concepts, Facts, and Feelings

Federico Reyes Heroles

Mexico, the United States, and Canada have entered into a free trade agreement, legally effective from the Suchiate River to the glacial regions of northern Canada, that affects approximately 380 million people. Sovereignty is a term that has been widely used in the debate over the North American Free Trade Agreement (NAFTA). But to understand the underlying social and cultural issues that, unlike tariffs, will not disappear with the signing of NAFTA, many levels of analysis must be considered.

Where, for example, does a country begin or end? "North America" is a term used to refer to the region formed by Mexico, the United States, and Canada. Central America and South America are other somewhat arbitrary descriptions. "Europe" and "European" allude to a cultural continent in which borders have been changing for centuries. The cultural diversity of Asia makes it possible to divide that continent into a thousand pieces.

Migration further complicates the issue of national identity: millions of people move, and will continue to move, from poor to rich countries, bringing with them habits and traditions from their home countries. It is also true, however, that these migrants adopt new ways of being and different codes for understanding human or social issues. A migrant becomes a new person, who leaves behind an original identity but, in the process, also affects the identity of the new country.

Mexico is technically a part of North America, but does it really belong in that grouping? And, if so, which Mexico? The Mexico of the north, with its vast plains that produce cereals, and where *mestizaje* is total or nearly total? Or southern Mexico, where different ethnic groups live in the same conditions as they did centuries ago and speak languages whose roots have nothing to do with contemporary Spanish? Although a river serves as the border between Mexico and Guatemala, the nearly 3,000-year-old Mayan culture is not contained by that river. Mayan religious ceremonies are conducted on both sides of the border,

69

and the indigenous peoples of the two countries see themselves as Mayans first and as Mexicans or Guatemalans second. From this standpoint, Chiapas and some regions of Oaxaca are as much part of Central America as they are of North America. But Mexicans from Nuevo León, Sonora, or Chihuahua, brought up with and accustomed to intensive trade and cultural exchange with the United States, have little or nothing to do with Mayans. Chiapas was the last state to join the Mexican federation, precisely because of its resistance to becoming part of what was a totally different world. The homogeneous, univocal, integrated Mexico is still an idyllic image even this late in the 20th century.

How does a businessperson or a laborer in a Monterrey steel plant or brewery view the economic interrelationship with the United States when every day trucks can be seen loaded with products leaving for the border? What arouses a feeling of sovereign feelings for the urban middle classes that use Japanese television sets and American cars and computers? What prompts sovereign feelings for the 30 percent of the "economically active population" still linked to the primary sector, particularly those involved in self-consumption agriculture, who will likely see their maize displaced by cheaper, imported grains?

This chapter will attempt to address these questions by looking at the different levels and types of sovereignty and how these levels play out in Mexico. First, however, it will be useful to examine briefly both the origins of sovereignty and then the diversity of Mexico.

Sovereignty: A Historic Perspective

Approximately four centuries ago, the universalist streams basically flowed from the papacy, and it was from this rationale that a concept of absolutist logic arose: sovereignty. Even though centuries have elapsed, tensions between universalist and anti-universalist conceptions still exist, evident in the conflicts over supranational agencies or the globalization of international trade and investment.

International law refers to treaties approved by countries that claim to be sovereign. The United Nations (UN) and other multinational institutions are the hybrid result of the "one country, one vote" doctrine and the imposition of historical reality. The creation of the UN Security Council and the veto power of superpowers have no doctrinal rationale. In fact, from this standpoint, the UN is quite schizophrenic—sovereign and collective entities subject themselves to conditionality that strips real power. Universalism is imposed, in part because of the globalization of economy and also for ecological, energy, and population reasons.[1] This interweaving of multinational and supranational agreements will undoubtedly increase—the international agenda already includes the environment, social welfare, gender issues, toxic waste, nuclear energy, migration, international capital flows, population, and a host of other topics.[2]

Proposals of a universal nature are not new. They have accompanied mankind throughout history, born from religious and millenarianist movements that lasted until late in the medieval period. Renaissance revindication was subsequently factored in, providing a territorial basis with a universal ambition. The next step was the Central European movement, particularly the French movement that gave birth to individual rights—as well as to the guillotine. The notion of social class was also universalist. The idea of manifest destiny is universalist and so are a large number of today's ecological movements.

It is difficult to condemn or approve universalism per se. Just as Christianity bestowed a superior standing on human beings during the barbarism of ancient times, it also paved the way for the Inquisition.[3] The declaration of the rights of man and citizens was the flag of the *Comités de Salut Public,* and that of Napoleon's, and was used as an excuse to invade half of Europe. Universalist ideas supported national socialism. It was universalism that led Soviet troops to invade their own allies and to attempt to destroy regimes. Consequently, universalism is not a question of principles but rather of concrete historical uses in a determined time and place.[4]

The external function of sovereignty (what Hobbes would consider power without rights) has been fundamental to the formulation of foreign policy by the United States (and other world powers). The doctrine of U.S. national security, for example, derived from U.S. desire to safeguard its interests to ensure that it would achieve the destiny it believed it deserved. In this sense, various U.S. administrations have discretionally identified those factors—a canal, another country's increasing arsenal, energy, or simply an ideology—that could impede the preconceived historical course that the country had set for itself. In an increasingly interrelated world the conditioning by, or subjection to, external factors is intensifying. Nothing suggests that sovereignty, as an ideology, will weaken. Sovereignty has cleared the way for what, according to common sense rather than theory or doctrine, could be called the right to interfere. The domestic and external functions of sovereignty intersect.

It is precisely within this standard of granted authority and real power that nation-states move. In the Mexican case, an ongoing struggle would remain because the formally granted power has been built on an extremely complex and rich historical reality that opposes the country's final integration. Conversely, for the United States the challenge lies in finding the formal and doctrinal support for the multiple acts of interference demanded by its very vulnerable and interdependent sovereignty.

The Many Faces of Mexico

Mexico's geographic integration has not yet been consolidated, social differences range from the miserable to the opulent, educational levels are a cause of deep concern, and the transition from an agrarian society to an industrial- and services-oriented one has not been completed.

Heterogeneity is part of Mexico's complex nature. The 1990 census classifies 70 percent of the population as urban, but many millions of these "urban" Mexicans live in recently created cities and are either peasants in the process of acquiring an urban culture or first- or second-generation migrants. In this sense, the so-called Mexican middle class is composed, to a large extent, of families that are in the process of changing from one way of life to another. As political actors, this group is only beginning to acquire a voice.

In contrast with the United States and Canada, where middle classes are traditional and steady, industrialization and urbanization in Mexico are still under way. The formation of a central Mexican mainstream is a very recent phenomenon. During the 1994 elections more than 35 million Mexicans voted, compared with just over 19 million in the 1988 elections,[5] and it is estimated that almost 40 million watched the televised debate among presidential candidates—Mexico's first such debate. Also, more than four million Mexicans went to the ballot boxes for the first time in their lives. It is apparent, therefore, that civic values are not yet fully consolidated throughout the national territory. According to the UN's Economic Commission for Latin America and the Caribbean (ECLAC), out of a total of 90 million

Mexican citizens, 40 million live in poverty and around 17 million live in extreme poverty; the average educational level is less than five years of schooling.

The relative youth of the population will be a factor in the country's political behavior. Nearly 36 percent of the population is under 15 years of age and 61 percent is between 15 and 64 years of age. The investment needed in education alone over the coming decades will be enormous. But the fact that more than 25 million students go to school every day implies that this generation has an unprecedented opportunity to acquire levels of information and knowledge much above those of their parents or grandparents.

For better or worse, these Mexicans, unlike their parents, are growing up with easy access to information about world events. It will be impossible for them not to make comparisons between Mexico and the rest of the world. The effect this will have on the political and social conscience of future generations is not known, but it is clear that these new citizens are growing up under unprecedented conditions.

Mexico is approaching the twenty-first century lacking full national integration. The daily rule of law with which citizens must comply is not questioned in Canada and the United States but continues to be a problem in Mexico. The role of a hegemonic force is still very much an unfinished matter—in Mexico, some of the issues to which Karl Schmitt referred as basic political decisions that support the constitutional and political order are still open to discussion.[6]

The principle of non-reelection, for example, was established in the Constitution of 1917 as a response to the frustrating experience with dictator Porfirio Díaz, who remained in power for more than 30 years. This policy, however, was extended to the national and local congresses and to the grassroots level of government, the municipal leaders. The strict application of non-reelection has led to a lack of professionalization in (and the weakness of) the legislative branches, the absence of a systematic evaluation of public policies, and the lack of continuity in programs. The consequent chaos results in urban disarray and an extraordinary waste of resources. This constitutional principle, and many others such as the relationship between the states and the Federation (particularly with regard to fiscal matters), have such importance and relevance that they actually cast doubts over the kind of rule of law that will finally prevail in the country.

Mexico is, in fact, in a period of profound redefinition. The constant amendments to the constitution and electoral codes imply a deep redefinition of the legal statute. Mexico is undergoing a transition away from an economy with autarchic intentions, an illiberal political system, and a state-oriented cultural project toward an open and interdependent economy, a real pluralistic party system (almost 25 percent of the population is already ruled by opposition parties, and competitiveness exists in approximately 64 percent of the country's municipalities), and an unprecedented cultural and information liberalization.

This digression might seem useless, but it helps illuminate the differences between Mexico and the United States and Canada. In Mexico, the difficulties of geographic, racial, and ethnic integration make the idea of nation as a political community far less important than it is in Mexico's two northern neighbors. The sphere of individual values is not subject to the idea of a superior interest that pertains to the political community known as nation. A national interest that transcends electoral campaigns, political parties, federated states, and minority interests has never been embedded in the civic conscience despite the fact that nationalism has prevailed in the Mexican political discourse for more than one and one-half centuries. In this sense, Mexico is not yet integrated as a nation—common people would find it difficult to decipher the expression "the nation, and the states." The natural and eternal link that imbues the Romantic concept of nation becomes fractured in Mexico because there never has been an original and deep racial, ethnic, and legal integration capable of forging a nation.

Levels of Sovereignty

Sovereignty is a complex term that contains many different dimensions. For the purposes of this paper, sovereignty has been broken into four levels, which, to complicate matters, overlap one another. The first dimension is the doctrinal, or theoretical, sphere, in which sovereignty is a conceptual construction and always tends to absolute terms.[7] Sovereignty at this level, for example, is related to the concept of the nation-state. The second dimension refers to political discourse, in which one finds the different political uses for the concept of sovereignty. Here, an attempt is made to attain popular consensus to consolidate support. In contrast to the doctrinal dimension, hermeneutic cleanliness and the strength of internal logic are less important here—

political discourse leads to a pragmatic use of expressions. The third level, factual, or absolute, sovereignty, goes back to the historical economic, trade, or ecological facts that are imposed on doctrine and discourse. In this respect, sovereignty does not draw from ethics but simply clarifies reality. The legacy of great empires and their colonies and economic and regional history depict this factual sovereignty, which has little to do with state ethics or the pragmatism of discourse. The fourth dimension is that of the subjective and refers to the feelings that a certain expression—sovereignty in this case—may generate in a determined population.

To understand what is happening in North America in light of the increasing interdependence among the three countries, it is necessary to analytically discern and separate these four dimensions.

Doctrinal Sovereignty

Doctrinal sovereignty derives from absolute terms that have little to do with the world at the end of the twentieth century. The origin of the word *sovereignty* is reminiscent of theocracies and conveys the image of an absolute, self-justified power. Sovereignty, as asserted in classical political theory, stands among the darkest terms. In concept, it confers an absolute decision-making power that it has historically lacked and that does not fit into a world that has a permanent, systematic, and incessant conflict over territories, wealth, or religious beliefs. These conflicts, and resulting adjustments, are noted in the written history of tribes, ethnic groups, principalities, and of nation-states, empires, and economic blocs. If doctrinal sovereignty truly had a direct and permanent effect on the international community, the map of the world would be static. That clearly is not the case.

Sovereignty as Political Discourse

Nationalism is a product of the discourse level of sovereignty. In Mexico, the image of the nationalistic citizen is well known. But given Mexico's heterogeneous nature, some might ask how such nationalism occurs.[8] The ideas of nation and nationalism have been used in Mexican official political discourse for more than a half century for many purposes: to explain the objectives of a centralized state, to guard the country from foreign interests (particularly the United States), and to revindicate an exclusive past that made Mexicans an incomparable sui generis case with regard to their family life, individual sense of humor, philosophy of life, and form of political organization.

Nationalism has been used to encourage and explain an art supported and financed by the state to transmit an ideology, to find abroad those to be blamed for the domestic situation, and to achieve goals established by an aloof bureaucracy that do not necessarily translate into an improved standard of living for ordinary Mexicans. Nationalism also has been used to explain the schizophrenia of a country with great natural resources that cannot systematically and permanently increase the living standards of its citizens and to justify an excessive protectionism and economic autarchy that benefits only a few.

Over the years, Mexican discourse on sovereignty has changed little, even as the other levels of sovereignty have advanced enormously. Most probably, the nation's history that is chronicled in official textbooks read by millions of schoolchildren conveys Bodino's concept of sovereignty (absolute, perpetual, indivisible, inalienable) and also the creation of the Mexican state as the starting point, a fundamental and willful act of the founding fathers. Most probably, Manicheism is still alive in those texts; the Spanish conquest is described only as an act by wicked men who came to steal wealth and nothing else; the Spanish perspective is not explained; and the numerous U.S. invasions of Mexico registered in national history, the diplomatic pressures exerted on revolutionaries, and the insatiable interest of the whole world, but particularly the United States, concerning Mexican oil and the Tehuantepec Isthmus are discussed at length. In this sense, Mexico's national history will not be much different from that of any other country. Villains and heroes play out their roles in accordance with that absolutist intention, based on sovereignty, that takes only self-interest into account.

Can official discourse stop resorting to the doctrinal concept of sovereignty and, consequently, elude Manicheism? As long as the concept of national history remains alive—and there is no indication that it will disappear—Manicheist versions will exist. These versions, however, are only a part of the emotional history of peoples. It will always be difficult for politicians or historians to elaborate an inwardly critical version of their own country. National history and political discourse are not self-scourging in Mexico—or in Germany, Argentina, the United States, or Japan.

For decades, the discourse of the ruling party and the center-left opposition brandished economic autarchy or isolation as the central element of nationalism and, consequently, of sovereignty. Changes in doctrines and discourse have not been easy, principally because prolonged financial adjustment, successive monetary crises, recession, and unemployment preclude discussing the advantages of an open economy. The benefits of open markets have not reached the poorest citizens, and segments within all political parties still advocate strengthening the domestic market, not liberalizing the economy, as the major economic goal.

Factual Sovereignty

Absolute or factual sovereignty lacks a concrete historical reference—it is much more useful as an analytical dimension. This type of sovereignty could be the highest authority in a world that increasingly appeals to multinational organizations for the regulation (or at least the attempted regulation) of those issues that are beyond any one government's control.

Mexico's factual sovereignty is exemplified by the level of trade between it and the United States. Mexico's economy may be 20 times smaller than the U.S. economy, but in 1995 total exchange between the two countries amounted to more than $100 billion. Just a decade ago, in 1986, it amounted only to about $30 billion. Globalization and close proximity to the world's largest economy have in fact imposed obstacles to real sovereignty despite the official discourse and despite, perhaps, popular sentiment.

A review of recent history supports the premise that sovereignty issues exist more at the discourse level than the factual level. During the last decade, since Mexico joined the General Agreement on Tariffs and Trade, the state has sold almost 85 percent of public enterprises considered closely related to sovereignty and has entered a free-trade agreement with a country that many considered to be Mexico's historical and symbolic enemy: all this without adverse public outcry or truly significant opposition.

Since World War II—in which Mexico discreetly participated with the allies—trade and political and cultural exchange between Mexico and the United States has increased steadily. In just over a decade, trade has more than trebled. Border-related conflicts between the two countries may be numerous, but this is not surprising given that the border is one of the world's most important, with hundreds of millions of crossings each year. In

1990, 274 million entries into the United States through its southern border were registered; of these, slightly more than one-third were U.S. citizens, which means that 173 million crossings were by foreigners. Throughout the 1930s, northward crossings totaled 225 million, 45 million fewer than in 1990 alone.[9] Moreover, the U.S.-Mexico border is the prototype of the meeting point of a Third World and a First World country, and is the longest of that nature. In 1994, gross production of *maquiladoras* was $25 billion.

It is estimated that in 1994 around 2.5 million trucks entered Mexico from the United States.[10] The Chamber of Commerce of Laredo, Texas, proudly announced that the city is the main point of entrance for U.S. merchandise to Mexico. Every year, thousands of Mexicans cross the border illegally to find jobs, but millions also go into the United States to shop, conduct business, or pursue travel and leisure activities.

Where, then, is the negative feeling toward "Yankees" if Mexico's major trade partner is the United States?

Interdependence increases from day to day. The effects have also been felt in what certain authors call "civil diplomacy," referring to the nongovernmental pressures, particularly from ecologists, human rights advocates, and the business organizations of both countries.[11] This civil diplomacy is now crossing the borders of North America to safeguard its own vested interests. These types of civic actions will thrive, in part because of their efficiency. In this sense, the central power of countries is decreasing, giving way to the emergence of interests that are not subject to sovereignty's internal or external logic. For example, as a consequence of the Chiapas conflict, different civic missions from both the United States and Canada have visited the region. Monitoring thus extends not only between governments but also between the societies themselves. This is a new and fervent phenomenon that leads to an increase in knowledge and linkages between the societies above and beyond any governmental endeavor.

Some of the characteristics of this new era are already present in Mexico: editorials in U.S. newspapers draw comment by Mexican radio and television networks only a few hours after their appearance; the Zapatista Army sends its messages via the Internet from the isolated mountains of Chiapas to New York in a matter of seconds—to attain an effect that transcends Mexican borders—and Mexican opposition groups participate in the forums of various universities and think thanks to express their demands and exert pressure from abroad.

Subjective Sovereignty

Nationalism is a necessary evil for the integration of a people's identity—all forms of nationalism have a potentially excluding nature. There can be extremely rigid forms of nationalism that appeal to racial, ethnic, or religious origins, as in the Middle East, and also more subtle forms, such as Saint Patrick's Day in the United States, an inclusive celebration based on a common origin. But the kernel of nationalism leads inexorably to one's own identification and, therefore, recognizes the boundary of what one is not. And that boundary precisely represents someone else. Appealing to one's own identity for the purpose of adding to collective efforts or attaining economic or political support is, in the end, a reminder that the "other" or "others" do not belong to the same community and that, in any given moment, they may oppose the group's common interest. Nationalism thus oscillates between recognition and denial.

Nationalism and sovereignty are, to a certain degree, two sides of the same coin. A uniform response regarding Mexico's relationship with the United States and Canada cannot be expected, of course, but it is useful to consider some recent opinion polls.

According to the 1990 version of the World Value Survey conducted by the University of Michigan, Mexicans are 4 percentage points less proud of themselves than their Canadian counterparts and 19 points less so than their U.S. neighbors.[12] It would then seem that Mexicans are perhaps rather ritualistic but not necessarily nationalistic. As part of their daily behavior, Mexicans have indeed learned to accept increasing interrelationships and the crumbling of many nationalist taboos. Two amazing facts are derived from the World Value Survey: in 1990, almost 60 percent of the population of Mexico accepted the idea of uniting with the United States if this meant a better quality of life; and 57 percent of Mexicans were in favor of establishing stronger economic links with the United States, and 66 percent favored such links with Canada.

Data from the United States and Canada are equally interesting: 64 percent of Americans favored a closer relationship with Mexicans, but only 54 percent of Canadians agreed. The study revealed that the highest degree of sympathy was from the United States toward Canada, with 82 percent favoring closer ties. People in metropolitan areas in Mexico, where better-informed social groups live, display a higher level of positive sentiments toward the United States than those living elsewhere. The higher the level of information and education, the greater the acceptance of the new status among the countries. In theory, then, if education and income levels rise in Mexico, resistance to greater integration would be overcome.

According to a national poll conducted by the *Los Angeles Times* in September 1991 and published on October 22, more than 56 percent of the Mexican population considered the performance of George Bush as good or very good, whereas the well-known opposition leader Cuauhtémoc Cárdenas, who shook the Mexican political system during the 1988 elections, obtained less than 40 percent in the same category. More that 49 percent of the population thought that foreign investment should be encouraged. Almost one-third of the population admitted having found employment in the United States, and somewhat more than 35 percent declared having relatives in that country. The poll confirmed the trend indicated by previous polls: approximately 55 percent of Mexicans have a good or very good impression of Americans, against approximately 20 percent who have a bad or very bad impression.[13] The favorable impression of the United States is not only far from negative, it has improved over time. In 1991, the *Los Angeles Times* reported that more than 72 percent of Mexicans had a good or very good impression of the United States. Japan ranked second, as in other studies, with 68 percent.

A long list of discursive insults, diplomatic mockery, and misconceptions regarding the attitudes of the Mexican people toward the United States has for a long time imbued the relationship between Mexico and the United States. It is clear that a more accurate and professional interpretation of what is happening between the two countries is needed. According to the *Los Angeles Times* study, admiration or sympathy toward Americans by Mexicans has a basis in the following findings: 22 percent of respondents valued the economic opportunities offered by the United States; U.S. democracy and wealth garnered 12 percent each; the next echelon of favorable responses, at 9 percent, referred to the U.S. cultural level, and good services and products and a government that protects people received 8 percent favorable responses. And what do Mexicans *dislike* about

Americans? Racism, 24 percent; drugs and crime, 19 percent; U.S. attitude of superiority, 12 percent; U.S. attempts to dominate, 12 percent; U.S. warmongering, 8 percent.

It seems at times that the diplomatic discourse of both Mexico and the United States has little to do with public opinion. In some aspects, the real links between the two national communities have extended at a quicker pace than anyone could have foreseen. In other aspects, however, there is still resistance. Opinion in Mexico is divided about whether Americans will be fair in their business deals: 45 percent are confident of fairness, while 47 percent believe Americans will be unfair.

Recently, several studies have revealed a strange reaction toward the financial package launched by the Clinton administration to help Mexico's ailing finances.[14] A high percentage of respondents believed that assistance should not be accepted, and an even higher percentage, well above 60 percent, affirmed that financial support jeopardized Mexico's national sovereignty. The weight of historical images continues to be important. For instance, the newspaper *Reforma* recently demonstrated how, on a scale from 1 to 10, Mexicans have the impression that the United States has more influence on Mexico than does the president of Mexico.[15] The Institutional Revolutionary Party (PRI), television, radio, representatives and senators, businessmen, newspapers, bankers, the army, labor union leaders, the Catholic Church, the National Action Party (PAN), judges, scholars, former presidents, peasant organizations, citizens, and finally the Democratic Revolutionary Party (PRD) were the other responses given, in that order, as factors that influence the country's everyday life. Thus, images play a fundamental role—they are frequently different from facts but as a collective phenomenon exist nonetheless.

Nationalism as an expression of people's sentiments can be stimulated by political discourse. But this is risky. The integration of North America, in fact and in people's sentiments, has progressed rapidly, although there also has been resistance to integration at the discourse level, particularly within the Mexican realm. The United States, however, also suffers from harsh and phobic attitudes that are not rational. Proposition 187, for example, is a monument to intolerance, and the southern border of the United States is a highly emotional issue in the United States because of Mexican migration. And while there may be little tolerance for the illegal migration of Mexicans (or individuals from any other country), it is not reasonable to ignore the

U.S. demand for this labor—that is, the U.S. population pyramid tends to be somewhat narrow at the base, which increases the demand for imported manual labor both to undertake the type of work not desired by U.S. citizens and to maintain the cost competitiveness of some products.

The consequences of phobias on both sides of the border are unknown, but nothing favorable can be expected. Mexican and U.S. pressure groups have been more nimble in carrying out their shortsighted actions than the governments have been in countering them. The danger of exploiting sentiments by using the sovereignty concept is that the result can damage the inevitably intensifying relationship between the countries. By making concessions to these types of pressure groups, the governments are actually allowing if not encouraging such groups to flourish. This body of misinformation, animosity, hatred, and deceit is the common enemy.

In any case, as information increases, national discourses might gradually lean in favor of comprehension rather than intolerance. Only through a deliberate policy of understanding will it be possible to attain a more balanced vision of facts among the North American nations. This approach, however, remains largely unexplored.

Conclusion

The encounter of Mexico and the United States could not be more exciting. It is impossible to guess what will result from a genuine encounter between such different societies, but it is clear that Mexico—and its NAFTA partners—is embarked on a reformulation of the meaning of sovereignty. The origins and purposes of the doctrinal concept of sovereignty were conceived for a very different historical moment, yet sovereignty remains the major articulating core of discourse among the three countries.

What kind of sovereignty will be exerted at the international level in years to come? Certainly it will be a sovereignty in which citizen and trade interests will maneuver in a domain that has nothing to do with the traditional respect for sovereignty as a country's untouched sphere of autonomy. Some think that it is possible to produce a limited list of issues that can be submitted for open international discussion, yet others believe the contrary. It is the author's belief that the linkages and interaction that are already occurring indicate that all matters will be subject to a certain amount of scrutiny. For instance, how can population, migration, and employment problems be considered separately from interaction with other countries? How can natural resources be considered a national interest when water, oil beds, and the pollution of oceans do not respect borders? How can a group of citizens, regardless of their nationality, be prevented from defending the right to life of a certain species? How can schools of fish be forced to respect the territorial waters of each country? A vast collection of international laws aimed at defending intersecting and interrelated interests of the different nations will emerge. Heightened international monitoring can become a new crusade of civilization.

It is not possible to imagine a social agreement without nationalism, for all forms of nationalism essentially stem from a certain degree of denial and rejection of the other party. It is possible, however, to encourage a less excluding form of nationalism, one that is more open and omnipresent and less phobic and ideological, so that forced cohabitation may ultimately be less conflicting.

The international scene has so many new formulas that even official identities are in flux. New long-term strategic alliances are replacing those of the cold war. Mexico, which not long ago was struggling for a resolution on the economic obligations and rights of the states, and which supported the causes of the so-called Third World countries, is now a member of the Organization for Economic Cooperation and Development. Have Mexico's socioeconomic variables changed to such an extent that it may now be considered a member of the group of the world's wealthiest countries? The answer is no.

If NAFTA is taken as a reference, it could be argued that Mexico belongs to the North, at least in formal terms. From the standpoint of socioeconomic indexes, however, Mexico is closer to the characteristics of the South, although a country of the South with an upper ranking. Even as far as demographic growth is concerned, Mexico is part of an intermediate scenario. Mexico's independent position and policy on certain delicate issues such as Cuba are recognized in international forums. In reality, however, Mexico is part of a new extended bloc integrated by the United States and the West.

The United States is also undergoing a process of redefinition. It remains the world's first power, but the advances made by Asia and Europe in trade should not be taken lightly. Mexico's integration with the United States is a positive development; however, it is important to note that the U.S. market of 260 million consumers is dwarfed by Asia's 2.1 billion. The United States has a strong interest in links with the rest of the hemisphere, in part because the new Asia and new Europe are formidable competitors; hence the invitation, issued first by President Bush and reissued by President Clinton, to integrate a hemispheric market of the Americas, from Patagonia to the northern glaciers.

Will history surprise us with the Americas of the twenty-first century as a conglomerate of races, ethnic groups, nations and languages; a conglomeration that, forced by globalization, will integrate a happy juncture of natural, financial, and cultural resources that permit strong competition with the rest of the world? If so, there may be new fields of study such as global economic law or no-nationality business administration. But even within that scenario, it is difficult to imagine that the concept of sovereignty, with its derivatives, possibilities, and risks, will vanish.

Notes

1. D. Dewitt, D. Haglunjd, and J. Kirton, *Building a New Global Order* (New York: Oxford University Press, 1993).

2. See *Our Global Neighbourhood, The Report of the Commission on Global Governance* (New York: Oxford University Press, 1990).

3. Leszek Kalakowski, *La Modernidad Siempre a Prueba* (Mexico City: Editorial Vuelta, S.A. de C.V., 1990).

4. A debate on sovereignty, particularly interesting because it was carried on among political actors, was published in the magazine *Este Pais*, April 1992. Particularly relevant was the participation of Miguel de la Madrid, former president of Mexico, Carlos Castañeda, former minister of foreign affairs, Hugo B. Margain, former Mexican ambassador, and Víctor L. Urquidi, Josué Sáenz, Antonio Martínez Báez, Adrián Lajous, and César Sepúlveda, among others.

5. Federal Electoral Institute (IFE), Mexico.

6. Carl Schmitt, *Teoría de la Constitución*, trans. Francisco Ayala (Madrid: Editorial Revista de Derecho Privado, 1934).

7. A useful theoretical and historical review of the sovereignty concept appears in F. H. Hinsley, *Sovereignty* (Cambridge: Cambridge University Press, 1986).

8. A critical and questioning text on the so-called Mexican nationalism is that of Teresa Warman, *Modernizacion en Mexico: Nacionalismo o Interes Nacional* (Mexico City: Alta Cultura, S.A. de C.V., 1988). A historical standpoint appears in David Brading, *Los Origenes del Nacionalismo Mexicano* (Mexico City: Ediciones Era, S.A., 1980).

9. David Loney, *United States-Mexico Border: Statistics Since 1900* (Los Angeles: University of California, 1990).

10. Banco Nacional de Obras y Servicios Públicos, *The History of the Roads of Mexico; Book 4, Recent Years* (Mexico, 1994), 125.

11. Julián Castro Rea, "Soberanía y Libre Comercio," *Este Pais Tendencias y Opiniones* 50, 1995.

12. *Este Pais*, April 1991.

13. *Este Pais Tendencias y Opiniones*, April 1 and May 2, 1991.

14. These studies were discussed in the January 30, 1995 issue of *Reforma*.

15. "Enfoque," political supplement of *Reforma*, April 16, 1995.

4

Economic Sovereignty in Mexico

Jonathan Heath

Mexican history might be characterized as a series of sovereignty issues because conflicts surrounding political domination explain much of what has happened in Mexico over time. At the core of all these struggles for political power, however, has been the economic domination of Mexico by a small ruling class. Most of Mexico's political battles have been consequences of attempts to retain this domination. Some have been struggles with forces abroad that have involved issues surrounding political and economic sovereignty. A good many, however, have been domestic disputes embracing power struggles within the ruling class.

First, it was the Spanish conquest and the Aztec fight for survival. The Spanish domination meant not only Aztec and Indian political submission but also their capitulation on economic, religious, and cultural values. During the colonial period, the Spanish caused an almost complete loss of economic sovereignty through their heavy mining exploitation and organization of the *Hacienda* system. Although independence from Spain meant a gain in political sovereignty for Mexico, it represented more of the same for the majority of the population: economic power remained in the hands of the ruling class, which consisted mostly of sons of Spaniards. The revolution at the turn of the twentieth century did little to change the roots of this economic domination, as demonstrated by the continued deterioration in income distribution.

In this sense, the concept of sovereignty has much more to do with power and domination than most politicians and policy-makers in Mexico have admitted. The average citizen or consumer is much more concerned with personal welfare than with an abstract concept. In most cases, a citizen is willing to sacrifice an intangible called sovereignty if it leads to economic gain, which is very tangible. Only if a citizen's personal well-being is affected by a lack of decision-making ability on the part of the government (caused by a lack of sovereignty) might there be protest.

In an all-other-things-being-equal situation, sovereignty matters. If one must choose between having and not having the ability to make one's own decisions, obviously the former is preferred. In the case of economic sovereignty, possessing the independence and power to make economic decisions is always better. In the real world, however, most decisions take the form of trade-offs. One may be willing to sacrifice sovereignty if the gain in economic welfare is sufficient. In the case of the ruling class and the political and economic elite, the trade-off is complicated. Usually, by giving up sovereignty, the ability to exercise power and increase wealth is sacrificed. The decision is therefore difficult.

But for the majority of the population, with its reduced per capita income and wealth, the trade-off is different. Giving up economic sovereignty starts to become an obscure issue when wealth and income levels are very low. When one is poor, there is little economic sovereignty to sacrifice.

The issue becomes complex once it is no longer an individual issue but a national one. Increasing sovereignty may decrease the ability of the majority of the population to increase its welfare. Most of these decisions, however, are not thought out in these terms, for when a ruling class makes a decision regarding sovereignty, it considers the effect the decision will have on the ability of the ruling class to retain its own power.

This situation is very apparent in the case of Mexico. Politicians have long used the concept of sovereignty to suit their own needs or to consolidate their power. They are much less interested in improving the welfare of the general population than they are in maintaining their own power and consolidating a system that permits them to exploit this power for their own well-being. The authoritarian nature of Mexico's political system has been absolutely necessary for this continued exploitation.

When Mexico was a closed economy, politicians talked continuously about the importance of sovereignty. The citizens were told that Mexico had the ability to make its own decisions and that the government was protecting the people from imports that threatened Mexico's jobs, culture, and general well-being. Not only was this line of reasoning used in all political discourse, it was imbedded in the official elementary school textbooks. Official history stressed the historical domination of Mexico by the United States, and the populace was taught that the geographical proximity of the United States was a curse. A well-known quote attributed to Porfirio Diaz nearly 100 years ago sums up this sentiment: "Poor Mexico, so far from God and so near the United States."

While the historical domination provides reasons to fear a major intervention and a loss of sovereignty, today it is more symbolic than real. During the past four or five decades it has been much less an issue of intervention (or loss of sovereignty) and more an issue of the possibility of politicians losing power. The basis of Mexico's political system is an obsession with control, and it may be attributed to the insecurity of Mexican politicians who continuously fear losing their domination. Nonetheless, this issue goes much beyond plain political sovereignty: sovereignty means power; power means control and domination; control means wealth and economic power.

The entire political system in Mexico has been based on maintaining control within a relatively small political elite known as the *familia revolucionaria* (the revolutionary family). Extremely powerful vested interests are at the core of this system. Not only do the politicians and their families make strong gains, but both labor and business leaders also have benefited enormously over time.

As a result, the disparity between rich and poor has grown worse: virtually any study focusing on the history of poverty in Mexico will show an ever increasing inequitable distribution of wealth. While most studies have shown that equitable income distribution has deteriorated in relative terms, some studies have even hinted at an absolute increase in poverty. The system induces those in power to accumulate wealth indefinitely, while it offers very little hope for the majority of the population. This is much the essence of the political problems present today in Mexico. Mexico may have had many different economic policies over time, but the structural imbalances have remained the same and income distribution has continued to deteriorate.

The political and economic systems lived off each other in a closed economy. When the administration of Carlos Salinas de Gortari began to change the economic structure, gearing toward a market-oriented economy, the power structure of the political system started breaking down. Behind all the political events that have occurred in Mexico during the past few years is an intense struggle between those whose vested interests have been deeply affected and who thus have much to lose and those who want to reform the system to allow a more democratic society in which the majority would have enhanced opportunities.

This is an issue of economic sovereignty. But it is an issue of the sovereignty of a privileged few versus the sovereignty of the majority more than an issue of Mexico as a whole. It is an issue in which corruption, impunity, and class privileges are at stake.

Although numerous examples exist to illustrate what sovereignty means in Mexico, probably the best example involves the North American Free Trade Agreement (NAFTA). Traditionally, the Mexican population has been told—by those who have wanted to maintain their power—that the United States is a country that could not be trusted. The official justification for a closed economy was sovereignty. When NAFTA negotiations began, the majority of the population supported free trade and concerns surrounding sovereignty issues were minimized and basically ignored. The general acceptance of NAFTA was grounded in the belief that the welfare of the majority would improve. If Mexicans could create more jobs, aspire to better wages, face lower prices, and have better product selection, economic sovereignty would increase. In such a case, who would care about political sovereignty?

This question, however, was answered quite forcefully in 1994 with the Chiapas uprising and the assassination of presidential candidate Luis Donaldo Colosio. In the case of Chiapas, a segment of the population that traditionally had been ignored seemed to be begging for attention and a stronger voice within the political system. In the case of Colosio, some people (most likely a small group representing the aristocracy who had lived off the previous system) feared that the reforms begun during the Salinas administration meant a loss of sovereignty, which must have been interpreted as a loss of power and control. Once it is understood that it is really *economic* interests that lie behind these struggles, it is easier to comprehend the current *political* power struggle: The current political elite simply have too much to lose.

What it boils down to is that throughout its history Mexico has paid an enormous price to attain sovereignty. Political sovereignty has been the excuse of Mexican politicians to ensure that they will retain their power and their personal economic welfare. Economic sovereignty has been used mistakenly as an excuse for government intervention, control, protectionism, and excessive regulation, all aimed at holding onto power. In the end, it is not clear that the economic welfare of the majority of the population has benefited.

True economic sovereignty increases with the welfare and the general wealth of a nation. In politics (in a democracy at least) one person means one vote. In economics, one peso (or one dollar) means one vote: the more money one has, the more votes or influence on economic decision-making one has. In short, the better job or the better house becomes attainable. In this sense, only the rich in Mexico can boast of any degree of economic sovereignty. As the economy grows and income distribution worsens, economic sovereignty is lost for the larger, lowest segment of the population.

In this sense, economic sovereignty for the nation as a whole must be examined side by side with measurements of income distribution. Before one can talk about a true increase in sovereignty—the ability of people to make their own economic decisions—an increase in the general welfare must occur, relative income distribution must improve, and the absolute level of poverty must decline. Otherwise, economic sovereignty would only apply to the sovereignty of certain groups (the political and economic elite) in the country.

Any system that struggles to maintain political sovereignty for a specific elite at the expense of a continuously degenerating income distribution loses much in economic sovereignty for the whole. In the end, economic welfare for a large part of the population hardly increases, which implies less economic decision-making (sovereignty) for the bottom half of the nation. Thus, economic sovereignty is lost for the very reasons that politicians argue that political sovereignty must be maintained: The freedom for the nation to rule itself is really an argument for maintaining power and not an argument to improve the general welfare. Mexico illustrates this quite well.

Historical Roots

Although the above argument implies that the sovereignty issue is overrated, it must be said that the fear of a loss of sovereignty—and the related mistrust of the United States—has deep roots in Mexico's history. The multiple invasions and interventions by the United States are taught in history classes in Mexico's schools. (All elementary schools in Mexico must use the official textbooks published and distributed by the Mexican government.) For example, the fifth grade history textbook has a complete chapter entitled "The American Interventions," which details how the United States invaded Mexico to annex half of Mexican territory.

Although the Mexican government prohibited U.S. families from settling in Mexican territory in the early years of the nineteenth century, the United States ignored this disposition. Families settling in Texas took advantage of a disorganized Mexican government and its lack of ability to enforce its laws in the northern portion of its territories. Then the United States adopted its "Manifest Destiny," which clearly violated Mexican sovereignty (and everybody else's) as a means to justify territorial expansion. While U.S. history portrays the Texan defense of the Alamo in 1836 as a heroic defense against an invading Mexican army, Mexican history depicts the same event as a clear violation of Mexican sovereignty, a total disregard for Mexican laws, and a heroic attempt by the Mexican army to defend its own territory.

History textbooks in Mexico portray the U.S. invasion of 1846 as an example of how the United States has no regard for other countries' sovereign rights and U.S. willingness to invade other countries at will. Textbooks picture the Mexican civilian population, including women and children, in the streets defending the city when President James Polk ordered the U.S. army to invade Mexico and take over Mexico City. When U.S. soldiers took over the castle at nearby Chapultepec in 1847, they slaughtered mostly young boys, some less than 12 years old, who studied at the military school located there. Mexican history teaches how the "boy heroes" wrapped themselves in the Mexican flag and jumped over a cliff, committing suicide to prevent the enemy from capturing the flag. Today one of Mexico's most important holidays is the "day of the boy heroes." In the end, Mexico lost more than half its territory, which today is known as Texas, New Mexico, Arizona, California, and parts of other U.S. states. Mexican textbooks finish this chapter by stating that it was "the nation's worst and most humiliating military and moral defeat in its history."

The history lessons of U.S. intervention, however, do not end with the U.S.-Mexican war. Almost all periods of Mexican history experienced recurring incidents involving the United States and its absolute disregard for Mexico's sovereignty. Another clear example was the U.S. support for Victoriano Huerta, the villain of the Mexican revolution of 1910.

The revolution of 1910 was a complex civil war involving multiple factions, in which all sides seemed to have fought against each other. Nevertheless, only one faction leader is an indisputable bad guy: Victoriano Huerta. The revolution started as an uprising against the 30-year dictatorship of Porfirio Diaz.

However, after Francisco Madero Gonzáles took over the presidency in clean elections in 1911, he was assassinated by Huerta with the full support of Henry Lane Wilson, the U.S. ambassador to Mexico.

President Woodrow Wilson believed that a democratic Mexico would be too independent and could thus oppose U.S. interests. As a result, Wilson supported Huerta in the assassination plot of Madero, Pino Suarez (the vice president), and Gustavo Madero (the president's brother). This pushed Mexico much further into the revolution and a decade of political and economic chaos. Again, history textbooks point out that the war brought with it hunger and epidemics that, when totaled along with war casualties, cost more than one million lives. The villains were Huerta and Wilson. Mexican history implies that the United States is responsible for a good many of these million lives.

After the revolution ended, the United States declined to recognize the Mexican government and its new constitution, which in Article 27 stated that Mexico had the sovereign right over its own subsoil, including the exploitation of all minerals and oil. The U.S. government wanted Mexico to exempt U.S. oil companies from this constitutional provision. Finally, in 1923, a secret treaty (the Treaty of Bucareli) was signed; in it the Mexican government provided guarantees to the oil companies, and the United States formally recognized Mexico. Historians consider this submission by the Mexican government as yet another clear example of the total disregard of the United States for Mexico's sovereignty.

Nevertheless, the tension between the two countries increased over the issue of oil. Mexican textbooks point out that in 1925 the United States almost invaded Mexico again in support of what was considered a highly aggressive and egotistic position held by both U.S. and English oil companies. Finally, in 1938, after years of great abuse, Mexico nationalized its oil industry. It was probably only World War II that saved Mexico from another invasion, as the U.S. government finally decided to support Mexico to avoid a major conflict on its border at a time when international conditions required attention in other places.

All Mexicans are taught these lessons in which Mexico suffered great losses in sovereignty, almost always at the hands of the United States. Thus, history provides an explanation for Mexico's overwhelming concern for the protection of sovereignty. This is why the oil industry has become a national icon representing sovereignty and independence, a symbol much more important to the majority of Mexicans than the benefits that could be derived from its privatization.

Many historians and politicians quickly point out the recent U.S. interventions in various countries (Panama, Libya, Bosnia, Haiti, Iraq, Somalia, and Grenada) to stress that U.S. attitudes and beliefs have not changed and to signify that Mexico is still under grave danger of U.S. intervention. Other current events, like the drug certification issue, are viewed along the same lines.

Foreign Direct Investment

Foreign direct investment (FDI) has historically caused much debate in Mexico, and governments have allowed varying amounts of FDI during different time periods. Periods that permitted increasing FDI have been followed by periods of expropriations and binding FDI laws. The Porfiriato era (1876–1911), for example, was very receptive to FDI and allowed large mining and oil exploration concessions to, mainly, British and U.S. companies. After the Mexican Revolution, however, both the oil (1938) and electricity (1960) industries were expropriated by the Mexican government.

FDI has been handled repeatedly as a sovereignty issue. FDI is allowed because the country needs the investment and foreign exchange and because FDI creates jobs and promotes growth. It is, however, seen as a threat to sovereignty because it allows foreign ownership and reduces the decision-making capabilities of the government. Historically, it has allowed situations to develop that later needed major corrective action (such as the oil expropriation of 1938).

In 1973, a very nationalistic FDI law that put strict limits on foreign investments and ownership was approved. Although this law was strictly binding regarding areas of possible ownership, it was more conspicuous for its complete lack of transparency. The law was deliberately ambiguous, relegating most decisions to individual government officials rather than setting straightforward rules. This nationalistic FDI law gave the government an excuse for not allowing certain projects while, at the same time, it gave a great deal of power to certain agencies and individuals that could authorize or restrict almost at free will. The obvious implications for corruption and favor buying were immense.

The sovereignty issue was clearly a power issue. The government needed a shield to protect itself, or certain close interests, from competition. If a personal economic gain could be made, however, the laws needed to be flexible. By granting final decision-making authority to individuals or agencies, the entire process became obscure and served the interests of individual government officials rather than society as a whole.

The entire process took on a ludicrous dimension when the regulatory framework, which allowed for concessions not permitted by the law, was approved. When questioned about the sustainability of the regulations in a judicial contention, the common answer was that that was how the Mexican system worked. It became clear that sovereignty was used as an excuse to consolidate power structures with little, if any, regard for true sovereignty.

One good example of the lack of transparency was in the 1980s when Apple Computer requested a license to open a factory in Mexico to manufacture computer hardware. Permission was denied under the framework of the FDI law. A short time later, IBM requested a similar license with a 100 percent ownership, which was granted. The decision process was so flexible that it put the entire system in doubt. Although the law was based on protecting the sovereignty of Mexico, the actual decisions had much more to do with corruption, graft, and power than with any true concern for sovereignty.

Today, as a result of the world's globalization process, the opening up of the economy to world trade, and an adoption of a more market-oriented strategy, Mexico's FDI laws have been renovated. Transparency and more leniency were injected into a different framework that tries to attract and develop FDI, instead of applying heavy regulation. Nevertheless, history has demonstrated that the legal setting for FDI has gone through a continuing cycle, which at times shuts out and at other times invites FDI. Behind this cycle lies the sovereignty debate, which does not seem to be permanently resolved.

External Debt

Antonio Ortiz Mena said, "The history of [Mexico's] external debt is the history of the life itself of Mexico."[1] Mexico gained its independence in 1821 and was born with an external debt problem. Since then, it has renegotiated its debt at least 18 times, suspended payments abroad 8 times, and repudiated part of its debt twice. With only two exceptions, Mexico has always recognized that it did incur its debt, even in times when it has not had the liquidity to repay.

The two occasions on which Mexico has not recognized its debt abroad were justified (from Mexico's point of view) by being illegally contracted. The first was the debt contracted by the French interventionist government of Maximilian, which was never recognized by the Mexican government of Benito Juarez. As a result, Juarez repudiated that debt in 1867. The second was the debt contracted by Victoriano Huerta after he assassinated Francisco Madero Gonzáles in 1913. After the revolution, this debt was repudiated by Venustiano Carranza Garza. In both cases, the debt was considered not contracted by a legal government and, hence, not violating the trust of a sovereign government.

External debt and Mexico's ability to service it have played a major role in its history. For example, England, France, and Spain landed troops together at the harbor of Veracruz in 1862 to force Mexico to pay its debt. Although Spain and England accepted the government's recognition of its debt and its promise to pay, France did not and instead decided to invade Mexico. Napoleon Bonaparte then sent the Emperor Maximilian to rule Mexico in 1864, opening yet another chapter in foreign intervention in Mexico.

The one outstanding period of sustained growth in Mexican history, with an average growth of more than 6 percent per annum for more than 40 years, coincided with the only period in which Mexico's external debt was wiped clean (as a result of the 1942 debt negotiation). Mexico had not been granted credit since the revolution of 1910 as a result of its inability to pay and partly because it failed to recognize the debt contracted by Huerta. After both the U.S. and British governments saw Mexico flirting with the German government before World War II, however, it was decided to condone nearly 90 percent of Mexico's past-due debt. The remaining 10 percent was given a 30-year payment period, with the first 20 years a grace period. With no debt overhang, Mexico grew more than 6 percent per annum during the following four decades.

The issue of contracting debt is predicated on a simple principle in business and economics—that of obtaining purchasing power today to generate a future revenue stream from which repayment can be made. It is difficult to think of progress in a society if credit is not readily available. There are additional implications, however, in terms of a government: A government can anticipate future spending to promote welfare, but it can also contract debt to achieve and consolidate power. If accountability is lacking, mismanagement and corruption will surely prevail.

Sovereign debt is different from normal debt. A standard business needs collateral to receive credit, while a sovereign government in most cases only puts up its ability to tax and raise revenue. Relative to ordinary private lending, sovereign lending involves higher costs when repayment cannot be made—the macroeconomic outlook is destabilized, causing unemployment, recession, devaluation, and inflation. It seems that the damage to the debtor country is far greater than the loss incurred by creditors.

Historically, Mexico's borrowing pattern can be characterized as a boom and bust cycle. Authorities borrow heavily to develop the economy; the ability to receive unaccounted-for resources usually leads to mismanagement; government goes into deficit spending and then looks for external credit to help finance its deficit; this leads to a balance-of-payments problem, which ends up in a devaluation crisis.

The pattern was modified under the Salinas administration. Large capital flows were attracted by private borrowing rather than through a fiscal deficit. The government, however, permitted a short-term debt structure based on the promise of far-reaching reforms. Given that the boom was built on Mexico's credibility, unfortunate political events and bad economic policy decisions (motivated by politics) led to the resultant bust.

Nevertheless, in the case of sovereign external borrowing, various issues come up. One issue is the motive behind the borrowing and the actual handling of the resources. In the case of Mexico, each administration lasts six years and its accountability is very poor because of its authoritarian nature. Instead of borrowing with a concern for increasing the welfare of the nation, governments borrow to consolidate the power structure and, in turn, their members' own personal wealth. The accumulated wealth of the political elite in Mexico is too obvious, while the origin of this wealth has always been obscure.

Some prominent politicians have been rather cynical about how the system works. Carlos Hank Gonzalez, a cabinet member in many past administrations, is reputed to have said that a politician in Mexico who remains poor is a poor politician. The root of the system allows the ruling class to make and bend the rules to continue accumulating wealth and power.

At the same time, the political structure offers strong incentives to borrow heavily abroad. Given that each administration lasts six years, cannot be reelected, will be remembered only for achievements within its government, and will not be held accountable for mismanagement, the incentive is strong to spend in the present on large infrastructure and other projects and postpone payments to future administrations. Present economic power increases at the cost of a future tax burden. These types of incentives help induce the boom and bust cycle.

Another issue at the core of external borrowing—especially when repayment becomes difficult—is sovereignty. Many argue that repayment of external debt should be suspended because foreign claims violate the sovereign status of the country. To a certain extent, this view seems ironic. A country borrows first to increase its economic sovereignty; that is, to increase its ability to grow and its power to decide which sectors or areas of the economy need development. After repayment becomes a burden, however, the debt's infringement on the country's political sovereignty is used as an argument against repayment.

Nevertheless, whether through scheduled payments or renegotiation, repayment has almost always been made. The biggest incentive for repayment, however, lies not in sovereignty issues but in the ability to borrow in the future.

Sovereignty and IMF Programs

At the core of the sovereignty argument is the role that the International Monetary Fund (IMF) takes once a country enters into a balance-of-payments crisis. As an international lender of last resort, the IMF imposes certain conditions on a country as a condition of helping solve that country's liquidity problems. In Mexico, as in many other countries, each IMF program involves a national debate surrounding sovereignty.

The conditionality in the IMF programs compromises key economic policy decisions such as the expansion of the central bank's domestic credit and the size of the government's fiscal deficit. This can limit the ability of the government to carry out public spending, change tax rates, and print money, among other things. The ability to make such policy decisions is the essence of a government's sovereignty. Mexico, like many other countries, has constantly battled the acceptance of an IMF program because of the political humiliation it causes.

Nevertheless, politicians ultimately have been willing to accept IMF programs so long as they have not disrupted the political system itself. The IMF may impose conditions but it does not impose accountability, especially for previous regimes that provoked the situation. In Mexico, it has always been the case that the necessity of an IMF facility has come at the start of a new administration as a consequence of the policy mistakes of the previous administration. The IMF's assistance helps the incoming government stabilize the economy and regain access to international capital markets—in other words, to regain economic sovereignty. Political sovereignty is only relevant to politicians when it enhances their economic power. If political sovereignty can be momentarily relinquished to gain economic sovereignty, it is more than justified.

The Power Structure and the Economy

The obsession for political control in Mexico is obvious in many different areas. One of these is the constant presence of discretionary regulations instead of straightforward, transparent rules. Such discretionary regulations allow the political system to transfer power to individuals instead of institutions while translating political power into economic gains. A system that concentrates economic sovereignty in individuals, however, must be careful in how it administers the transfer of this power. This is why the decision-making is concentrated in a highly centralist government.

Although the Mexican constitution outlines a federalist government, in practice almost all decisions are controlled at the center. The president removes governors at will; almost all tax collections are carried out by the federal government; state participation is controlled through a revenue-sharing scheme; and almost all public enterprises are federal. The president therefore has nearly absolute control over who makes decisions and who receives what and retains ultimate power within the system.

Sovereignty at the state level is limited to whatever the center is willing to relinquish. Once relinquished, however, the same system of power defines the state's control over municipalities. At the municipal level, local power is distributed along the lines of a small fiefdom. For each level of government to take maximum advantage of its power, regulations exist at each level. While this multiplication of regulations and controls makes normal business practices quite difficult, it guarantees the power structure.

All businesses in Mexico know how the system works and have adapted accordingly. Excessive regulation does not stop economic activity, it just forces it to function differently; that is, through individuals in government, not institutions of government. Thus, a businessman establishes a relationship with a government worker, who solves the firm's problems. Although the loss of efficiency is tremendous, political power is translated into economic gain.

The development strategy that had been employed since the early 1940s was to expand an incipient industrial sector in a country whose nature was predominately rural and agricultural. While the classic infant-industry argument was used to justify a highly protectionist scheme with strong subsidies, it also encouraged a political structure that could promote growth while guaranteeing the continuance of the power structure. The industrial growth that followed brought with it a rapid urbanization and a quick displacement of agricultural employment in favor of both industries and services. In spite of the strong industrial growth, however, the combination of very high population growth and rapid urbanization made it very difficult for the industrial sector to create enough jobs. Thus, the service sector appeared as a residual absorber, although with very low-paying and highly unproductive jobs. The result was an increasingly inequitable income distribution.

When Luis Echeverria took office in December 1970, it was felt that the government should take a much more active role in the economy, with a primary goal of improving income distribution and reducing the absolute level of poverty. Public expenditures increased without a countervailing increase in revenues, causing inflation and external imbalance through a growing current account deficit. In the end, the government was willing to try to help improve the economic welfare of the majority of the population so long as the power structure remained untouched.

The protectionist nature of the import substitution model created very large rates of return on domestic investment and production compared to export activity, which achieved low rates of return because Mexican products could not compete in international markets. As a result, exports as a percentage of gross domestic product (GDP) decreased consistently between 1940 and 1982. The steady decline in export revenue forced Mexico to return to the international community to borrow to finance its growing current account deficit. The result was an end to the era of little or no external debt and a return to an increasing debt-service burden.

Acting in what seemed to be its newly defined role, the government started to increase dramatically the number of public enterprises. To reduce unemployment, the government viewed its obligation as buying any firm or business that was going bankrupt, or creating new firms. Public tariffs and utility fees were kept low to prevent any hardship on the aggregate of the population. Wages and salaries of public employees were raised as a means of improving income distribution. Regulations and controls appeared in almost every segment of economic activity as the government expanded its power structure and its ability to extract benefits from every transaction.

No revenue adjustments were made to accompany the expenditure outlays, and the public deficit increased rapidly. At the same time, the financing of the current account became more difficult and foreign exchange reserves started to dwindle. Finally, in 1976, after 22 years of a fixed exchange rate, Mexico had to face a currency devaluation. With this came a serious questioning of an economic structure that had been modified to help the lower and middle classes and to improve income distribution. Improvements, however, had been virtually absent.

At that moment, it was obvious that Mexico needed to implement strong structural changes. The previous strategy had worked for more than three decades but was no longer viable. What was needed was an approach that could generate foreign exchange to finance a growing demand for imports and complement a low domestic savings rate while, at the same time, inducing efficiency in the industrial base.

Although the industrial base had grown vigorously for the previous three decades, it had done so at a tremendous cost in efficiency. Instead of opening up the economy by using export-led growth, Mexico relied on large new oil reserves in the midst of increasing world oil prices. Although oil revenues helped Mexico grow for five more years and created extraordinary leverage for foreign borrowing, oil revenues only postponed the necessary structural changes. What had been seen as an invitation to increase economic sovereignty by reducing dependence abroad turned out to be precisely the opposite.

When oil prices fell in 1982, at a time of record-high world interest rates, the Mexican economy found itself in a situation much worse than it had faced in 1976. Both inflation and the public deficit were much higher in 1982. The current account deficit and the debt service burden were far above previous levels. The number of public enterprises had risen, along with the number of unproductive state employees. Economic sovereignty seemed to have dwindled, reducing any maneuvering ability necessary to overcome the ensuing crisis.

Unfortunately, the government responded to the financial crash of August 1982 with measures that complicated Mexico's recovery and its possibilities for structural change and strongly undermined faith in the authorities' ability to overcome such adverse conditions. Dollar-denominated bank accounts were frozen and forcefully converted into pesos at an exchange rate lower than the market rate. Foreign debt service payments were temporarily suspended while a renegotiation was forced on the international banking community. Exchange controls were introduced and private banks were expropriated. Public confidence was exhausted, creating great capital flight.

Thus, Mexico faced the enormous necessity of initiating major structural transformations in 1983, coincidental with the new administration of Miguel de la Madrid. A strategy was needed to reduce both the fiscal and external deficits and also find a viable source of foreign exchange that would not only permit Mexico to continue to service previous debt but also allow it to return to sustained economic growth.

Up until this moment, economic growth had been sufficient to hold off major criticism of a political system that ruled out accountability and permitted the elite great leverage. In the absence of economic growth, however, opposition started to appear both within and outside the political structure.

The logical choice was a liberalization of the economy: the elimination of price distortions, export barriers, and government intervention. The shift to a more market-oriented economy, however, was much more complex than originally perceived. A good part of the necessary changes involved deregulation and less control, which was a major threat to the political structure. As a result various debates took place inside government circles.

One topic was the relationship between economic and political reform. Could the economic structure be reformed without major changes to the political system? Should the economic reforms precede major political changes or be applied simultaneously? Could superficial or cosmetic political changes suffice? In the end, the government decided to go forth with economic reforms while holding back on political changes, most likely because although most leaders were convinced of the necessity of economic changes, few wanted to see an end to the political power structure. If the reforms failed, the political structure guaranteed that the elite would retain power.

The other debate concerned the pace of the economic reforms. Should Mexico open all markets through a type of shock treatment, or should opening be gradual? If liberalization were gradual, which markets should be liberalized first? How much liberalization was necessary? At that time, 1983, the government decided to apply only some of the reforms and at a relatively slow pace.

Many questions emerged in a society that had been heavily controlled by the state for decades. The political system of elites that feeds on these controls and regulations to retain the power began to weaken as the processes of deregulation and liberalization started to diminish the government's grasp on power, all the while facing enormous opposition from within the existing structure. Thus, Mexico initiated its first phase of structural change with intimidation and questions about what, where, and how it was going.

It is hard to find substantial improvements when examining economic statistics between 1983 and 1987. While inflation averaged 101.9 percent in 1983, at the end of 1987 it was 159.2 percent. The public deficit represented 16.9 percent of GDP in 1983 and 16.0 percent in 1987. Growth for the period averaged -0.3 percent per year, and foreign debt was restructured three times. The financial crisis deprived Mexico of all voluntary international lending and forced the economy to maintain a current account surplus to finance its capital account. The resulting exchange rate policy of a sustained undervalued currency exacerbated inflation. This meant that Mexico maintained a steady capital transfer abroad, which limited domestic investment possibilities. In short, the reforms were going nowhere.

Although certain structural changes were initiated in 1983, it soon became apparent that both the pace and scope were limited, which did not reestablish confidence. The privatization process began slowly and was limited to irrelevant firms. Deregulation was unconvincing and fiscal retrenchment was unsuccessful. Uncertainty about the direction of and commitment to reform during this process of slow change only delayed policy action. Lack of results hindered further advances. Finally, after the market crash of October 1987, the government reconsidered its strategy and initiated a heterodox stabilization program, which led to a much more aggressive structural change. It was finally decided that a very rapid trade liberalization was preferable to a gradual process for reasons of credibility and long-term efficiency.

In December 1988, when Carlos Salinas de Gortari took office, the government initiated a much more aggressive structural change strategy. Confidence and renewed credibility emerged at once. For the first time since the financial crash of 1982, Mexico received capital inflows and a promise of a development strategy that could be financed. It was soon learned that a consistent macroeconomic strategy along with market liberalization attracted capital. It seemed that Mexico had finally found its course.

Nevertheless, part of this strategy involved a closer relationship with the United States and what some perceived as a compromise of Mexico's sovereignty. What exactly did Mexico have to give up to gain better access to the U.S. markets? The biggest mistake made by the Salinas government at that moment was not so much surrendering sovereignty but rather concentrating more on the end product than on the transition process.

The costs of large-scale reforms were basically overlooked. It was forgotten (or rather ignored) that sweeping reforms would result in the closing of many inefficient industries, with consequent unemployment. There also would be a significant time lag before new, more efficient industries would start to appear. Moreover, these new industries would have considerably different skill requirements. Considerable protracted unemployment would surface with a high political cost. Although the final gain in efficiency was badly needed, the cost to achieve it was never correctly measured.

An open border increases the pressure to become efficient and competitive, and firms struggled immediately to reduce costs and increase productivity. The easiest cost to reduce, when emerging from a highly protectionist scheme, is the labor overhead: firms will try to produce the same output (or more) with fewer workers. Thus, during the transition period between a closed and an open economy, the job generation capacity of the economy is reduced considerably. As a result, most of Mexico's growth between 1989 and 1994 seems to be explained by productivity increases rather than by job generation.

This negligence about the costs and implications of the transition process has cost Mexico dearly, not only in the peso crash in December 1994 and its effects on economic activity, job destruction, and general welfare but also in the credibility of the necessity of the economic reform process in itself. Mexico is now clamoring for a more accountable political process, and this in itself might be the most important step that the country can take to achieve true economic sovereignty.

The Move toward Democracy

However objectionable the Mexican political system has been, it has worked for decades. Some contend that part of the explanation lies in the traditional submissive role of the Mexican Indian and mestizo. Others have offered explanations involving the low educational level of the general population. Others say that after a century of instability characterized by continuous *"planes y pronunciamientos,"* the population welcomed and accepted the stability brought about by the Institutional Revolutionary Party (PRI).[2]

The general acceptance of the political system coincided with a long period of economic growth. The system only began to break down once economic growth disappeared. Previously, the government dealt with problems like the student uprising in 1968 by absorbing the leaders into the PRI and giving them political positions. Superficial changes were made to contend with most criticism; for example, Echeverria's policy of a more active role for government as a response to unequal income distribution.

The drive toward economic sovereignty had been characterized by a closed economy with excessive government regulations. Protectionism had led to a very high rate of return on domestic investments and a very low incentive for exports. As a result, non-oil exports as a percentage of GDP saw an uninterrupted downward trend from the early 1940s to the mid-1980s. This meant that the natural supply of foreign exchange was increasingly scarce. As a result, the government turned to external debt until the debt service burden became overwhelming. The economic crash of 1982 not only represented the beginning of an international financial crisis but also marked the end of a decades-long economic model.

The resulting reforms that were implemented beginning in the mid-1980s marked the beginning of changes that were much bigger and more complicated than the Mexican government had anticipated. Mexico adopted the so-called Washington consensus policies that called for privatization, fiscal retrenchment, trade liberalization, and deregulation, all aimed at implementing a market-oriented economic strategy. Although the economic reasoning behind the reforms made sense, the transition problems involved were either underestimated or basically ignored by Mexico's government.

First, the economic and political systems were designed to complement each other, guaranteeing that the economic power was maintained by the ruling class. By changing the economic structure through deregulation and less government control, both the economic and political systems were undermined. The political structure, which fed on regulations and controls, found itself in a weaker position facing the possibility that it could lose power. The economic sovereignty issues, which were always very different for the political and business elite than for the majority of the population, started to change. With the economic reforms, the majority of the population could start aspiring to improve their welfare, while the traditional political class was facing a possible abdication of power.

Economic sovereignty, from a national viewpoint, has not yet gathered enough force to become a major issue in itself. Although topical issues have surfaced since the implementation of NAFTA (two examples are trucking and tomatoes), the debates have not attracted the attention needed to become dominant issues. The domestic struggle to reshape both the economic and political structure of Mexico, however, makes headlines almost daily. Debates on issues such as the desirability of neoliberal policies or an established rule of law are taking center stage. In many ways, it seems that Mexico is being reinvented.

Many changes have started to appear as a result. For example, at the beginning of this decade the middle class started growing and acquiring debt. This segment of the population started believing that it would soon achieve First World status as a result of the economic reforms. The changes were not applied to the political system, however, and these very reforms started clashing with the traditional political structure. The devaluation of 1994 resulted in a quick end to these beliefs.

The struggle between the traditional political structure and the new, market-oriented economic system has pushed Mexico further into a transition period from which it is not known when, or how, the country will emerge. A move toward a more democratic regime, a slowdown of the current reform process, and maybe even a reversal of market policies are all possible. In the end, a major overhaul in the political system will be necessary if the economic changes implemented during the past decade are to survive.

President Ernesto Zedillo has shown strong intentions of trying to revamp the political setup. Until now, it has seemed that the size and scope of the necessary changes have been simply overwhelming for one man. Because Zedillo is an outsider—not a member of the *familia revolucionaria*—he has been able to focus on the problems differently from his predecessors. For the same reason, however, he has not been able to build sufficient consensus for change within the system.

One recent example underlines the difficulties ahead. At the beginning of 1996, leading up to the preparations for the PRI's national assembly, a group of more than 200 PRI congressional representatives signed a document for discussion, which was really a disguised petition for change. Although the document attempted to address multiple issues to be discussed as the party's platform, the economic model introduced by Salinas came under direct fire. The document specifically calls for a change in the current "neoliberal economic system."

The document in itself demonstrates the same ambiguity that faces the entire country. While it calls for reducing inflation, increasing trade, stabilizing the currency, reducing interest rates, and balancing the fiscal budget (all elements for the current economic strategy), it also calls for further state intervention. In the end, the document seems to call for a reversal of anything associated with the Salinas administration while it recognizes the necessity of reform.

Final Note

Although a new order will appear eventually, neither the time frame nor the final product can be foreseen. It is hoped that the new order will provide not only a more democratic scheme with a market-oriented economy but also a system that no longer promotes inequitable distribution of income. This implies a system in which economic sovereignty becomes a true national issue and no longer has different meanings for different segments of the population.

Notes

1. In Jan Bazant, *Historia de la Deuda Exterior de Mexico 1823–1946* (Mexico City: El Colegio de Mexico, 1968), Prologue. Antonio Ortiz Mena was Mexico's finance minister from 1958 to 1970.

2. During the previous century, each overthrow of government was initiated by a "plan" or "pronouncement" enunciating a new scheme.

5

Sovereignty Political

Charles F. Doran

Sovereignty in North America

One of the hang-ups the United States possesses regarding sovereignty is that it knows that small countries can accede to the obligation to transfer some authority over trade matters to a bilateral or multilateral dispute resolution process more readily than the United States can. Although these partners are not giving up much because they never exercised much unilateral authority over trade matters in the first place, the smaller partners share equally in the benefits of a more efficient, and perhaps more fair, trade dispute resolution process.

The origin of the problem lies in a theoretical debate regarding sovereignty and equality examined subsequently in this chapter. First, however, it is useful to distinguish between internal and external sovereignty, a point also developed more fully later. Internal sovereignty is the capacity to exercise domestic control over matters that affect a population and territory. External sovereignty involves freedom from external control—it implies foreign policy autonomy.

When states are highly unequal in size, the large states yield more sovereignty than do the smaller states through interdependence arrangements because, in the absence of mutual dispute resolution, large states depend on their weight to get their way in trade terms more frequently than could the small states. ("Getting their way" ironically may mean yielding to special interest groups in their own polity at the cost of the larger interest of consumers as a whole, a point rarely made among political analysts.)

A further hang-up is evident concerning the procedures and outcomes of ongoing dispute resolution within the Canada-U.S. Free Trade Agreement (CUFTA) and now within the North American Free Trade Agreement (NAFTA).

Members of the bilateral dispute panels are randomly chosen from an agreed roster of candidates contributed by each country. Approximately 80 disputes have been considered by the joint panels under both CUFTA and NAFTA auspices. To the general observer, the process seems to be working well; but to the specialist, looking more closely at procedures, there is fear that the panelists may in some cases be prejudiced in favor of their own country's cases. If this suspicion proves correct, bias could undermine the dispute resolution process.

All of this came to a head in the softwood lumber case, easily the largest, longest, and most tortuous case to come before the CUFTA.[1] Although we cannot go into the details here of the 11-year history of the case, a case that was penultimately decided by a three-member panel of the Extraordinary Challenge Committee composed of two Canadian and one U.S. judge, the sense in the business community on both sides of the border is that politics entered the decision-making. There is little proof. The decisions made by the panels did, in fact, break down along the lines of national membership. Ultimately, the decision was made outside the bilateral dispute resolution context. Canada was to limit itself to a 32 percent market share. The pact was to stand for five years.

This is a bad precedent. Should voting on the dispute panels, especially in critical cases, again occur along national lines, the U.S. hang-up in favor of unilateral decision-making on trade would surely reemerge. Objectivity and neutrality must, therefore, be ever more carefully observed in future trade cases. Moreover, the decision to move outside the dispute panel context and opt for a managed-trade outcome augers poorly for the NAFTA framework.

For differing reasons, Canada and Mexico are delighted to see the United States cede a certain amount of sovereignty on trade matters but are not, in the U.S. view, terribly enthusiastic about a tighter trade and investment community.[2] Both Mexico and Canada see NAFTA as a way of securing access to the huge U.S. market. Conversely, partly because the Mexican and Canadian markets are so much smaller than the U.S. market and the trade benefits cannot be of the greatest significance for the United States, the United States looks at Canada and Mexico in terms of industrial and commercial location as much as trade. Politically, the United States believes that Canada entered NAFTA largely as a defensive measure so as not to lose the benefits of the earlier CUFTA.[3] The U.S. perspective on why Mexico accepted participation is that Mexico needed capital for development and saw the association with the United States as its developmental ticket into the twenty-first century. The road was a lot rougher than any of the participants expected.

Politically, some in the United States suspect that Canada has been campaigning for an expansion of NAFTA on grounds that new members would act as a counterweight to the U.S. presence. At least this position has appeared in speeches by Canada's trade minister, speeches oriented toward domestic political consumption and calculated to gin up support for the treaty and perhaps for Canadian foreign policy more generally. Mexico, too, has a long-established fear of U.S. dominance. NAFTA is a sharp break with this instinctive set of past feelings driven by the confidence of Mexico's young technocrats, now a little shaken by the peso devaluation of December 1994 and by the political events surrounding former president Carlos Salinas de Gortari. But the United States does not want to put pressure on the Mexican or Canadian economies for additional mutual trade and policy concessions at this time. Nor does the United States want to move on the accession of Chile or other South American governments so that the standards and intent of NAFTA are in any way compromised.

The U.S.-led rescue of the Mexican peso using oil-backed loans has brought a reality home to the United States. Regardless of political intention on each side of the border, creation of a trade area is a slow, difficult business that is made more complicated by the inclusion of countries at very different levels of economic development.[4] Under no circumstances at present are the American people politically ready to underwrite any more international trade and commercial bargains at the level of financial expenditure of the Mexican financial rescue. The response of the European Union and of Japan to this rescue is very similar in attitude despite (or perhaps because of) the currency scares that the Europeans themselves have experienced in the preceding two years. From now on, trade area creation on the part of the United States will need to proceed on the assumption that political infusions of confidence will not include large dollar outlays in the form of back-up loans. Americans look at their own external sovereignty quite differently after the peso crisis than they did before.

The problem facing the United States in terms of external sovereignty, with implications for trade and commerce, is twofold. One aspect is the propensity to slip into protectionism in an attempt to augment external sovereignty. Abuses of antidumping legislation in some cases and of voluntary export restraints (VERs), such as those employed in the softwood and lumber outcome, are good examples of this problem.

The other problem with external sovereignty in the age of the World Trade Organization and of NAFTA-generated binational trade dispute resolution machinery is the shortcoming posed by trade theory and bargaining practice. Protectionism in neomercantilist countries, best exemplified by Japan, is like an onion: Rip off the outer layers of tariff barriers and underlayers composed of nontariff barriers of great intricacy and equivalent impenetrability remain. The modern theory of protectionism cannot account for these barriers, and contemporary techniques of multilateral trade negotiation cannot eliminate them. In an age of dynamic gains to investment promoted by the multinational corporation, lack of access to principal markets is debilitating.[5] Neomercantilist markets exist because of well-established, government-supported techniques of collusion among domestic firms that divide among themselves markets usually closed to foreign investment.[6] Neomercantilist markets in countries like Japan, South Korea, and China as a matter of calculated strategy and empirical evidence are also far less likely to buy imported manufactured goods than are traditional liberal economies. The consequence is that the neomercantilist economy is not subject to traditional liberal economic interpretation or to General Agreement on Tariffs and Trade (GATT) procedure. Bargaining becomes increasingly bilateral and coercive.

It is unfortunate that the effort to guarantee shares of a market such as Japan's through managed trade arrangements is a poor way of achieving access to the neomercantilist economy and appears preferential to other partners. Hence the dual problem of unilateral slippage into protectionism coupled with inability to guarantee mutual trade and investment access in a world of neomercantilism is the greatest present-day external challenge to sovereignty in North America.

The internal challenge to U.S. sovereignty, self-imposed, is the low rate of saving, the dwindling relative rate of investment in civilian research and development, the too-low rate of increase in productivity, and the consequent poor showing in terms of economic growth. Among the Organization for Economic Cooperation and Development countries in the 1980s, for example, the United States found itself in the middle in terms of average gross domestic product growth, well below Japan and even Canada. In the end, the United States hurts itself because of its own bad policies far more than foreigners can hurt it with their policies.

Sovereignty Gained, Constrained, Reconsidered

Will North America form a single political entity? Will the United States, Canada, and Mexico form a common market? The simple answer, at this writing, is that they will not. Sovereignty is not the only reason why they will not, but it is one reason.

In its cycle of relative power, the United States finds itself in a dual position.[7] Each side tugs at the foreign policy role from a different direction. In absolute and relative power terms, the United States is the most powerful state in the system, in both economic size (though no longer in per capita income) and virtually every component of military strength. But the United States is past its peak of relative power and is very gradually entering a downward trajectory. Given the collapse of the Soviet Union, the former fact of seminal absolute and relative power drags the United States toward a very large, perhaps exclusive, foreign policy role. But the latter fact of declining relative power encourages the United States to husband its strength and to pick its foreign policy responsibilities more selectively.

On the one hand, the reality of seminal power invites the United States to stress its external sovereignty and to avoid concessions to other governments with respect to trade dispute resolution or any other area of major policy harmonization within North America. On the other hand, gradual movement down its cycle of relative power causes the United States to take interdependence more seriously. Its near neighbors become more important to it on a global scale. It is more willing to bargain on matters that affect its external sovereignty.[8] Thus its current position on its power cycle sends dual signals that pull in opposite directions but that the United States must take seriously.

What are the U.S. hang-ups regarding sovereignty? To get beneath political rhetoric that only muddles this seemingly elementary question, we must first examine the meaning of sovereignty, its historical origin, and its relationship to other competing notions. For instance, do sovereignty and security amount to the same thing? National security is regularly invoked as a justification for restraints on trade. Is this action an abuse of sovereignty?

Similarly, notions of equality impinge on sovereignty. If all states are looked on as equal subjects of international law, one conclusion may follow. Sovereignty, for example, may be regarded as easily shared and transferable. If states are viewed as members of an inexorable systemic hierarchy, in which power is an important commodity, quite another interpretation of sovereignty will follow.

Finally, sovereignty and productivity relate to each other in complex ways. Does sovereignty constrain productivity? Can economic productivity enhance sovereignty? U.S. attitudes toward sovereignty will be regarded differently depending on how these questions are answered and where the trade-off between these concepts lies.

What this analysis will show is that political sovereignty is a concept that is deeply value-sensitive. Moreover, it is a subject that has changed as to locus within the polity and as to political meaning across time. Without consideration of this theoretical and historical framework of connotation, any discussion of political sovereignty becomes misleading. Viewed from the political perspective, whether the United States has hang-ups regarding sovereignty depends very much on the philosophical presuppositions that the examiner brings to the question.

Modern political thought is, in large part, a search for the locus and meaning of sovereignty. What makes this quest so engrossing is that, historically, the search was far from a simple linear venture. It was not a mere one-way drift from the barren heights of the absolutist state to the fertile valley of democratic liberalism. Medieval Europe had earlier been the home of the Hanseatic city-state, the Italian city-state, and feudal constitutionalism. Each had set limits on sovereignty not known by the absolutist state and not revisited for a half millennium. In the rough-and-tumble of Machiavellian Europe, the quest for political sovereignty was intense and led in many directions.[9] Empire also rested uneasily next to state.

The Meaning of Sovereignty

At its simplest, sovereignty is an idea with two sides. First, sovereignty has an internal side that implies supreme power over the internal workings of the polity. Sovereignty from this perspective means the capacity to exert control over a population and territory. This definition is akin to that offered by international law, at least since Grotius.

Second, sovereignty also has an external side, meaning freedom from external control. By this definition sovereignty affirms the autonomy or independence of the state.[10] External sovereignty involves the capacity to govern without outside interference, implying that other governments are not allowed to impinge upon, or affect, the decision-making of the state. The state is a political island surrounded by friendly oceans that separate the state from peers and rivals.

It is easy to see that the first definition is essential to the second, and vice versa. For example, civil war occurs when internal sovereignty is in contention—little or no internal sovereignty is also the technical circumstance known as anarchy, or the absence of government. The state, however, may enjoy external sovereignty in cases of either civil war or anarchy: other governments may forgo intervention, allow civil war to burn itself out, or waive the temptation to institute a government of their own preference to fill the internal political vacuum posed by anarchy. In other words, other states in the system may honor external sovereignty regardless of the internal condition of the state. Yet without internal sovereignty, external sovereignty does not a state make.

Conversely, a state lacking external sovereignty is crippled and dysfunctional. A state that can command the support of its people and can govern its entire territory but is beset by foreign threat is a state whose governance is incomplete. Regardless of whether foreign impingement involves political meddling or actual military invasion, the absence of external sovereignty— the absence of autonomy—undermines the capacity of the state to govern. In both Canada and Mexico there is fear of this kind of extension of economic and political influence from the regional center; that is, from the United States. This is why both states were quick to reject the so-called hub-and-spoke model of integration in which influence and trade ties emanate from the hub to each peripheral actor through a spoke, but with little contact across spokes. Thus, the smaller actors would not have the capacity to balance the greater weight of the hub. Bilateral treaties with the United States were quickly rejected in favor of one encompassing, multilateral agreement among all the partners— NAFTA.

Another application of Canada's and Mexico's fear of loss of external sovereignty concerns the problem of extraterritoriality. This problem took renewed form in the U.S. response to the shooting down of the U.S. planes piloted by two American-Cubans in international waters off Cuba: U.S. legislation penalized the branches of U.S. firms in both Canada and Mexico doing business with Cuba. By constraining the branches of U.S.

firms abroad doing business with Cuba, the United States sought to tighten the embargo against Castro. But extraterritoriality extended to foreign firms as well if they dealt in expropriated properties in Cuba. Because neither Canada nor Mexico shared with the United States the same strategies of coping with Castro, these actions by their larger neighbor were sharply disputed.

Autonomy is sometimes equated with identity.[11] But political autonomy is more than a sense of belonging to one polity (identity) and not to others. Autonomy is the facilitator of political opportunity and permits a government to formulate and implement policy regarding subject or citizen. Without autonomy, internal sovereignty becomes an extension of the foreign policy of other states and, thus, is itself negated.

Sovereignty as a unified concept must possess both the internal and the external dimensions. Yet the dimensions are not substitutable or identical. Plenty of governments have the autonomy to act but lack the internal muscle to do so. Still others possess the internal machinery of government and the will to act, but imperialism or direct military threat undermines the capacity or, perhaps, the courage to govern.

Historical Origin of Sovereignty

Building Up Sovereignty

Much of political philosophy, historically, involves the effort to gain or enhance sovereignty in the attempt to make it more effective or far reaching.

In his advice to the prince on how to augment sovereignty, we observe the quintessential Machiavelli: "A prince therefore who desires to maintain himself must learn to be not always good, but to be so or not as necessity may require . . ."[12] That is, sovereignty is increased by the double standard for state and citizen. States will do what citizens morally cannot—states can cheat and deceive while a citizen doing the same would be put in jail. The Protestant theologian Reinhold Niebuhr made famous the same advice in terms of foreign policy, highlighted in the title of his book *Moral Man and Immoral Society.*[13] Perhaps the most important issue that separates twentieth-century political idealists and realists is the extent to which the state is freed from the bonds of international law, opinion, and morality; that is, the extent to which sovereignty is exempt from these expressions of constraint.

While recognizing that the prince was answerable to God and to natural law, Jean Bodin argued nevertheless that the prince was the locus of sovereignty within the state.[14] The citizen was subject to the "sovereign" and obtained his legitimacy through the prince. The sovereign was not legally accountable to his subjects although they were certainly legally accountable to him. This attitude contrasts sharply with ancient Celtic law, for example, or early medieval law, in which the lord had a deep responsibility to his vassal once that vassal had declared his fealty and once that fealty had been formally acknowledged by the lord.[15]

Bodin and other writers of the fifteenth and sixteenth centuries were codifying political theory and law that justified the supremacy of the prince inside the absolute state. This development of political theory clearly enhanced the internal sovereignty of the state in the name of the sovereign. The notion of external sovereignty, while assumed, was less formulated.

Writing during the English Civil War and near the end of one of the bloodiest wars of the early modern period on the Continent, the Thirty Years War, Thomas Hobbes epitomized the fear of loss of external sovereignty and constructed his theory of sovereignty as a result.[16] Hence, like Machiavelli who strove to defend the prince from the foreign aggressor, Hobbes erected the Leviathan to halt the invader at the gate. The Leviathan state was intended to be so awesome in power that it was capable of defending a population and territory against foreign conquest as much as against internal civil war. Domination by the sovereign was endured because the alternative, war and invasion, was so horrible that any order was virtually an advancement over no order at all. For Hobbes, self-preservation was at the core of his notion of sovereignty. Because life in the state of nature was "nasty, brutish, and short," life inside the Leviathan could only be an improvement.

In his lasting contribution to political thought that went far beyond absolute monarchy, Hobbes claimed that the state, and indeed society itself, was an artificial construct. The individual was the atom of social and political reality. It followed that the state had no existence that was meaningful independent of the individual. This was a revolutionary idea that eventually would undermine the unlimited power of the state. If Hobbes gave political theory the foundation of argument that would eventually limit the power of the state, however, he also gave political theory the instrument that would maximize that power at the cost of subject and foreign monarch alike. According to Hobbes, law required the power of sanctions against the rebellious or criminally inclined citizen. Enhancement of the power of the prince was essential to the preservation of the Hobbesian state. Institutions alone provided no security for the weak. Only institutions girded with power were capable of defending the Leviathan.

Loosening and Constraining Sovereignty

From Locke and Rousseau through the Madison papers to the modern constitutions of Germany and Japan, the task has been to limit the powers of the sovereign in the name of the citizen. Using the individual as the counterpoint to the prince, the government has gradually been expected to devolve powers on the citizen. This achievement has occurred in a number of ways institutionally and in terms of legal remedy.

The greatest single innovation in democratic process that sets this form of government apart from dictatorship is voting a government out of power and the willingness of government to step aside when the citizens so indicate. This principle is facilitated greatly by the existence of multiple political parties (though not too many for ease of coalition-building) such that an organized political opposition exists and an organized shadow government is quickly able to assume power when duly elected. Domestic sovereignty is nowhere better devolved toward an electorate, and refined, than through this principle of electoral rotation.

In the U.S. system, a balance of powers has ensured that not one sovereign, but three, coexist at the federal level. By offsetting the powers of the legislative and the judicial with that of the executive, no branch is capable of becoming paramount. This constitutional reality is the negation of the idea of absolute sovereignty. Nonetheless, modern democratic theory can still be read as a search for the locus of sovereignty inside the state.

Parliamentary democracy places sovereignty within a cabinet that is held to be responsible to the legislature in which the members of the cabinet themselves serve. Not satisfied with this statutory locus of internal sovereignty, modern comparativists have devised behavioral techniques to discern where power lies—within the parliament or within the executive—and whether the democracies themselves are converging or diverging in policy aspects.

In practice, other factors within society and within the state may be equally important in determining the locus and disposition of internal sovereignty. For instance, a strong free press has been described as the cornerstone of democracy. It is perhaps the principal domestic institution in contemporary Russia that stands between a drift toward dictatorship or mafia rule and an orderly evolution toward more representative government. Likewise, the barometer for slippage away from democratic rule in Latin America, for example, frequently is the clampdown on a free press.

The gradual extension of the franchise during the nineteenth century from the male property owner to every male adult and to women and minorities is a devolution of sovereignty toward the individual that is matchless elsewhere in terms of effect. Without access to the voting booth, no individual can claim adequate political representation.

Internal sovereignty has been regularized as much as it has been contained. The principal vehicle for regularizing sovereignty and ensuring fair treatment is a system of law and an independent judiciary. When the modern state is contrasted with the Leviathan, no aspect of the contrast is more striking than that expressed by law and the judiciary.

Finally, interest groups vie with the citizen and with government for power in the modern democracy. The advent of the organized interest group capable of effecting legislative change, as well as electoral difference, is perhaps the least understood and most potent form of discipline on the sovereignty of government associated with modern democracy.[17] Tocquevillian in conception, the voluntary interest group continues to affect governmental sovereignty in practical terms in each of the major democracies. The existence of interest groups competing for influence is a way of fragmenting governmental dominance and therefore of sharing domestic sovereignty.

In looking at the devolution of sovereignty away from the absolute government, the movement toward limits on centralized power has been inexorable. Yet true democracy is neither old nor certain. It is buffeted by internal challenge in much of the Third World today, not the least in China. The emergence of a large, informed, politically active commercial middle class seems to assure the perpetuation of democratic reform and, therefore, the constraint on domestic sovereignty. This middle class is attentive to the preservation of liberal opportunity. A truly successful market economy and highly centralized political authority are a contradiction. The Soviet Union exemplified this political-economic contradiction. Conversely, a polity composed of individuals who own nothing and, therefore, are unconcerned about the defense of fiscal and monetary responsibility and individual freedom as well, perhaps, is a very soft floor on which to build representative institutions and safeguards to governmental usurpation of power. Ownership reinforces responsibility and control, the two instruments necessary to offset the potentially oppressive power of government. Institutions themselves cannot guarantee liberty. Only the capability and initiative of the individual citizen can make representation work.

The Political Redistribution of Sovereignty

A further pattern of change regarding political sovereignty is its redistribution within the polity. Federalism involves the complicated sharing of power across regions and levels of government within the modern state and today is regarded as an essential means of bringing government closer to the users of services.[18] The large bureaucratic state has made federalism ever more necessary. Similarly, the emergence of assertive regionalism in polities like Belgium, France, Spain, the United Kingdom, and Canada, as well as in a host of developing countries, beckons federalist solutions for the sharing of power territorially. In Canada, the separatism of the Parti Quebecois government perhaps challenges this concept of federalism most directly. But some of the same resentment of the center is felt in different ways in British Columbia and in Alberta. Over time the same kind of regionalist sentiment might emerge in northern Mexico through affiliations with the conservative National Action Party (PAN) and the problem of alienation from Mexico City.

Redistribution of sovereignty can occur any time in a state's history. No formulas exist for its workability. But several observations pertain.

- No net increase or decrease of sovereignty occurs. Sovereignty is merely moved up or down politically or moved around geographically across levels of government. Because constitutions are difficult to change, shifts of sovereignty often occur in terms of legislative acts or executive policy decisions on small issues. Seldom is there a formal declaration or constitutional revision that reorients sovereignty in a massive way.

- A redistribution of rights (demands) should be accompanied by a redistribution of responsibility (obligation to generate revenue). This problem was felt in Mexico among the public universities outside the capital city where responsibility and financial revenue seem to move in opposite directions. Similarly, the Reagan administration strongly favored a redistribution of services to the states, but there was not always a corresponding redistribution of taxing powers. The states found themselves assuming new responsibilities for welfare and health care without always obtaining a diminution of federal tax powers and a corresponding increase of their own tax powers. A gap between rights and responsibilities is always an upsetting possibility accompanying a redistribution of sovereignty. Whether the U.S. governors will get federal help to deal with educational, environmental, and social welfare costs or only the right to solve these problems is very much at the heart of current Senate reform efforts.

- One measure of where the distribution of sovereignty actually stands in a polity is the identification of the entity that has the power of taxation. Control normally accompanies the power to tax. In the modern state, however, regions and subnational governments have sometimes obtained the right to spend without having to raise the corresponding revenue. These smaller units of government have received "block grants" to spend as they like, or, as in Germany and Canada, "transfer payments" from richer to poorer regions of the country. Similarly, in Mexico, Mexico City exerts great authority over the distribution of tax pesos regionally. A struggle then occurs over how many restrictions ought to accompany the right to spend.

- In states with a strongly federal character, higher levels of authority must work out systematic procedures for meeting with the usually more numerous lower levels of authority. Sometimes these meetings take on the character of administrative barter far from electoral control. Governors' conferences in the United States regularly address the administration in Washington. First ministers' conferences in Canada bring together the 10 premiers of the provinces with the prime minister. This procedure for decision-making has been dubbed "executive federalism" and has addressed seminal matters of policy for the country including massive revisions of the constitution (Meech Lake conference) and the distribution of revenue from oil and gas production. Similarly, behind the effort to deal with the Chiapas rebellion in Mexico and the "contract with America" budgetary reforms in the United States is an attempt to work out a new intermediation politically between states and federal governments.

• The redistribution of sovereignty raises two large questions: (1) at what point does the federal executive so relinquish its powers (regionally and/or subnationally to lower levels of government) such that the federal government is unable to govern, and (2) at what point does the country itself begin to fragment, especially where natural cultural and linguistic fissures exist that reinforce separation? These are difficult questions to answer abstractly. In theory, there are clear limits to the degree that internal sovereignty can be redistributed to other jurisdictions before the capacity to govern declines and the cohesion of the state snaps. But where these limits are, and how they vary with differing societal circumstance and institutional framework, are poorly assessed subjects. Empirical models of sovereignty redistribution ought to be developed and applied to states within the contemporary system.

Sovereignty and Competing Notions

Political sovereignty is not just a matter of addition, subtraction, or redistribution as examined in the first section of this essay. It is also a matter of sovereignty in the context of other important competing matters. This issue will be assessed in the following section.

Sovereignty versus Security

It would be an oversimplification to imply that external sovereignty is synonymous with the security of the state. Sovereignty encompasses all foreign effects on a state; security involves protection against military invasion or loss of vital interests. Examples may help clarify the distinction.

Suppose that a country like Canada is bombarded by the radio and television signals of a large near-neighbor from across the border in Buffalo, New York. The country has been made to forgo some of its opportunity to enjoy peace and quiet. One might even go so far as to say that the U.S. signals have impinged on Canada's sovereignty to the extent that Canada's own programming is now less popular because of alternatives available from across the border. (A dissenter might point out that the country's citizens are now actually better off because the scope of their choice of programming has been increased.) Moreover, some of the country's own stations probably lose advertising revenue. The country could, therefore, possibly be said to have "lost" some sovereignty because its government has less control over the menu of programming that its citizens watch and hear. Yet, in the end, the technological innovations of television satellites and the Internet probably undermine the most creative efforts of a policy to isolate its citizenry. Iran is finding this. Why should not a much more enlightened and interconnected polity like Canada as well?

Has that country lost security? The answer is negative, by this definition of security. The country is not in danger of being invaded militarily because of exposure to foreign programming. Of course, the situation would be different if the purpose of the programming were somehow to intimidate the population or to "soften it up" preparatory to an actual military invasion. But this purpose is absent from the content and orientation of the programming. The country's military security is not one bit more threatened by the existence of the foreign broadcasting than if the broadcasting had not occurred. Foreign broadcasting, by this argument, does impinge on some aspects of the sovereignty of the country, but foreign broadcasting is not a threat to its military or territorial security.

For instance, if one holds that the ideology and values of the United States are hostile to the culture one is trying to implant in the Canadian population, say for the purpose of generating a common feeling of Canadian national identity, then the exposure to foreign broadcasting could perhaps be held in some minor way to be threatening. Similarly, the affected country could make the claim that its own broadcasting firms are losing advertising revenue because their audience is reduced by the foreign competition. This loss of revenue, it might be said, undermines the economic vitality of the stations that carry more national content in their broadcasts and thus reduces their effectiveness in conveying a message of national identity or unity. Under certain extreme circumstances, therefore, some critics of foreign broadcasting could probably claim a low-lying threat to their culture and, eventually, to the will to resist foreign aggression. But this security argument would still seem very strained. The more plausible argument against foreign broadcasting in this admittedly unique historical and political example would still necessarily be the sovereignty argument. Having a unique and vibrant culture and different language than English, Mexico seems aloof from these very Canadian arguments.

Now that the difference between sovereignty and security has been established, the question becomes how these behavioral conditions have changed for most states over time. It is the author's belief that the security of most countries has increased over time. In the nuclear age this proposition may be far from obvious. The assertion, however, is twofold.

First, in the Middle Ages, war was a vocation, an annual activity that was associated with the lives of the male aristocracy. Even the aristocracy in nineteenth-century Mexico shared some of these preferences. As states became better constituted, and as other interests came to compete with war for the attention of governments, invasion was less common. As a statistical matter, controlling for the number of states and for time, the borders of most states today are simply less subject to violation than they were historically.

Second, in the special case of states such as the United States and the Soviet Union with second-strike nuclear capability—nuclear capability sufficient to withstand an all-out nuclear attack and still respond with overwhelming nuclear force—their nuclear power has made them virtually impregnable. They cannot be successfully invaded. The nuclear stalemate deters aggression. Of course, they are not secure from either accidental nuclear war or nuclear terrorism, however likely or unlikely either might be, or suicidal nuclear attack, again discounting this outcome because of the improbability of its occurrence. Moreover, if such outcomes did occur, the cost might be higher than anything previously experienced, at least in terms of absolute losses. (Entire city-states, of course, have been destroyed by war in the past, raising the relative costs to 100 percent).

Do not mistake these arguments for pacificism or for the obsolescence of war. That the risk of war has declined for most states does not mean that major war is impossible (e.g., a war over Taiwan could break out between the governments in Taipei and Beijing, or a war between Russia and China could occur regarding border differences) or that if it occurs the losses will be lower than that already experienced this century. Because war is less likely for most states does not mean that their defenses are less important. For most states today, however, the interval of peace separating war-involvement is greater than in the past and will probably continue to increase. War unfortunately is as great a threat to security as it ever was, taking fully into account the amount of damage major warfare in the future could do to civilians as well as to belligerent nations, a dichotomy virtually erased in many kinds of warfare today. And even though war in North America is unthinkable, a war involving North American troops is far from inconceivable outside the region. U.S. and Mexican forces now undertake some of the same joint training exercises long conducted by the U.S. and Canadian militaries.

Although security has probably increased for most states in the system today, external sovereignty overall has not increased because of the enhanced security of the nation-state. To make that claim, one must consider all other facets of external sovereignty contained in this broad and difficult-to-encompass notion.

Sovereignty versus Equality

There is no logical or theoretical reason why sovereignty and equality should be related as concepts at all. Yet in the polity they may find an intriguing and even imperative relationship. Equality has a bearing on sovereignty in an immediate way.[19] Sovereignty may have an impact on equality in a fashion that is more indirect but still meaningful politically.

Equality is important to the functioning of state independence. Controlling for other influences, political equality among nation-states (nominal equality) will make the expression of independence easier. Equality that is grounded not only in international law (as a right) but also in the structure of the international system (in the relative power of states) will facilitate the manifestation of autonomy. Imperialism will be less likely in a system that is characterized by little hierarchy or, at least, little

inequality of power. Coalitions and balances will emerge to reinforce the independence of states. Also, the struggle to defend
independence will be rendered easier by the presence of other
relatively equal powers sharing an interest in the preservation of
a system of autonomous nation-states.

The impact of sovereignty on equality is more complex.
Great external sovereignty will ensure that a state is able to run
its internal affairs virtually unaffected by political currents elsewhere.[20] Such a state has the capacity to make decisions for
itself. Should that state choose programs that encourage greater
internal political and economic equality, it will have the opportunity to put those programs into effect. The revolutions in
France, Russia, and China come to mind as examples. Without
external sovereignty these societies in tumult would have been
overrun by neighbors fearful of the consequences of the revolutions for themselves. The revolutions led to greater political
equality of the respective citizenries, shielded by that external
sovereignty, however much other harm the revolutions did to
these societies.[21] Although there is no necessary correlation
between greater external sovereignty and the propensity to generate internal political equality, the absence of external sovereignty certainly would have squelched the great revolutions
attempting to impose political equality on peoples.

A government with a high degree of internal sovereignty
may attempt to impose political equality on society. That certainly was the situation under Stalin and Mao Zedong. On the
other hand, historically, absolute monarchy certainly did not
encourage social equality in Europe. Absolute monarchy seemed
to increase the distance between classes, especially between the
aristocracy and the commercial middle class. Distance between
the monarch and the respective social classes could be used in
many ways, some of which seemed to strengthen the state at the
cost of the upper classes, as was true under Louis XIV of France
and under Henry VIII of Britain.

But whether greater social equality emerged because of the
existence of heightened internal sovereignty or in opposition to
that enlarged sovereignty is a matter for historians and empirical
political scientists to judge. "The least egalitarian countries,"
wrote Peter Drucker, "are those that have tried hardest to redis-
tribute income: the Soviet Union; the United States; Great Britain."[22] This statement of course implies that more egalitarian
states like Sweden, Norway, Canada, and Japan are more egalitarian *because* they have not tried to be, a hard proposition at

best. What can be said here with some confidence is that increased internal political sovereignty created the opportunity for strong-willed governments to act precipitously, sometimes with the intention of destroying economic and social inequality, although the motivation and the techniques used by these totalitarian governments often damaged the societies cruelly. Other values suffered correspondingly.

Sovereignty has the capacity in both its external and internal dimensions to affect political and social equality. Equality of states has certainly shaped the capacity of those states to preserve a decentralized international system (i.e., their external sovereignty). Sovereignty and equality are thus fated to require joint assessment despite the seeming desperateness of the conceptualization that underlies each primary notion. Whether NAFTA will increase or decrease equality among the three countries is an interesting question. The author would suggest that it will somewhat hasten greater equality although the United States will not be overtaken in terms of economic growth by either neighbor. Similarly, over time, as markets are allowed to work more naturally, NAFTA will be helpful in reducing internal economic inequality in each of the three countries, especially Mexico.

Sovereignty versus Productivity

Modern neoclassical economics makes the assumption that, if resources are allocated properly without artificial impediments to the flow of capital and labor, efficiency is likely to result and the growth in economic welfare is likely to be maximized across the international system. For international political economy, however, another question is posed. Instead of wants or utilities, productivity here means the more efficient and dynamic generation of new output. This is productivity involving a high degree of individual initiative and collective entrepreneurship. What is the relationship, if any, between sovereignty and the productivity of the individual?

It is easy to argue that too much sovereignty, either internal or external, is the enemy of productivity. A system composed of individual political units, each with a high degree of external sovereignty, is likely to be structurally heterogeneous, politically competitive, and prone to interunit jealousy. Coalitions may form, but overall political cooperation across all of the units, such that economic competition will be allowed to function unimpeded, is likely to be hard to constitute. Switzerland may be a counterexample but only because of its very elaborate rules of coordination and constraint. Such a state system will be hard put to yield mutual gains from productivity. The impediments to trade and perhaps to the movement of capital and labor will prevent the pooling of resources, and few economies of scale will be possible. Labor will not be able to maximize its acquisition of specialized skills in small markets. Technology will not develop rapidly and most assuredly will not be applied to output as quickly or thoroughly in a fragmented world market. Because of the high barriers to capital mobility, the diffusion of technique will stagnate. The commitment to a high degree of external sovereignty undermines each state's capacity to enhance its own productivity. Although these generalities may be deemed overstatement, they are not, especially where a polity is small and therefore unable alone to generate much internal specialization. Relative gains stand in the way of absolute gains, for both state and system.

Now consider some examples of cases with high internal sovereignty. All of the recent cases of extreme internal sovereignty have been among the Communist states—the former Eastern Europe, the former Soviet Union, Cuba, and Maoist China.[23] China became economically more productive only when it relaxed much of its internal and external sovereignty. But these countries may be of a societal type inherently hostile ideologically to the market; the fact of their monumental internal sovereignty has been of secondary importance in explaining their lack of productivity.[24] Moreover, productivity did exist in the military sphere and in educational endeavors, in that pure math and science thrived (but, realistically, perhaps as an intellectual and social refuge from the brutality of the rest of society for the relatively few and privileged practitioners).

But consider other examples of both high internal sovereignty and relatively low productivity; for instance, the Latin American countries. Here of course low real per capita income is a contravening variable.

Some may argue that Japan is a contrary case, yet in reality Japanese internal sovereignty is very diffuse across the prime minister and elected officiate and is pronounced only within the bureaucracy. Most successful economies are overseen today by governments in which the powers at the center have been curbed. In essence, this is the idea of trade dispute resolution as expounded in NAFTA to which all three North American business communities have acceded.

For a more compelling assessment, we ought to look at those cases in which internal sovereignty is low but productivity is not especially pronounced either. After controlling for per capita income and size, very few examples come to mind. Britain, Australia, and Canada all complain about level and growth of economic productivity. When their productivity is considered more broadly in educational terms, however, their record is impressive. In formal economic terms, their productivity is still substantial.

It is hard to escape the conclusion that societies with a democratic form of government that diffuses sovereignty politically and with a liberal social order in which the middle class has an important share of power are societies that also enjoy the greatest productivity. But this conclusion in turn generates an additional question about the causal relationship between sovereignty and productivity. Does the diffusion of political sovereignty, internal and external, cause an increase in productivity, or does such diffusion only create a social and entrepreneurial environment that is receptive to productivity gains? Is a setting of diffused political sovereignty sufficient to increase productivity, or is it merely necessary? These may seem like philosophical nuances, but these questions in fact get to the heart of the problem concerning productivity in the modern polity.

Productivity will flourish if it is given the right political environment, an environment in which high internal sovereignty does not smother it, and high external sovereignty does not cut it off from the external contact that is essential for it to flourish. But is that enough? Is productivity totally self-generating and spontaneous? Or can it be nurtured? And if productivity can be nurtured, how is this to be accomplished in the context of sovereignty that is kept within bounds but is perhaps also turned to the advantage of the propagation of productivity? This subject is too little studied by those who have come to the same conclusion as has this article, namely, that sovereignty loosened but still under fetters is more generous to productivity than is sovereignty unconstrained. Within the set of countries in which sovereignty is conducive to productivity, how is productivity best advanced? Will some of these societies create a more positive environment still, an environment that will not only unleash productivity but propel it to previously unknown heights of achievement?[25] NAFTA has attempted to achieve these goals through the conventional neoclassical economic goal of enlarging a market so as to increase the profitability of economies of scale and other efficiencies.

Sovereignty Transformed

On the eve of Columbus's departure for the New World, the two most successful organizations were the Roman Catholic Church and the empire—the so-called Holy Roman Empire and the Ottoman Empire. The former was about to contend with the largest test of its more than 1,000-year tenure, the Protestant Reformation. The empires were about to face the challenge of new territorial administration and consolidation.[26]

A half-millennium later, the two most successful forms of organization are the state and the firm. Who knows what new types of organization are about to contest them. They are, of course, quite busy contesting each other.

The only church that is still defiantly secular in its political presence is Islamic fundamentalism. It appears to be a recrudescence of ancient fervor now misplaced in the modern world of materialist governance and Western values. Empire, on the other hand, appears safely dead since the collapse of the contemporary world's most self-conscious empire, the Soviet Union. Empire died not primarily because of an internal inability to govern but because it no longer paid for itself. In the past, empire at the center lived off empire on the periphery in the context of colonialism and under the tutelage of the navy. Although not all colonies were prepared to pay taxes (the American colonies) and many did not pay enough to remain interesting (Canada) and thus were sloughed off in the age of free trade, the heyday of France and Britain corresponded to the maturation of the paying colony.[27] More recently, however, "colony" exacts tribute from the "colonizer." The Soviet Union subsidized Eastern Europe with oil and the purchase of shoddy goods, not the other way around. Although scarcely imperial, the United States subsidized wealthy Japan and Western Europe in terms of military defense. With this juxtaposition goes the enthusiasm for imperial conduct or an overly extensive defensive role. Today empire is too expensive.

Gaining from all of this, of course, is the entity that has eclipsed empire, the nation-state. It has done so largely because it has perfected both the internal and the external determinants of sovereignty better than any other organization. Today the state controls a monopoly of force. It mixes internal and external sovereignty better than church, empire, multinational firm, or supranational organization such as the United Nations. If Europe unites to the point of becoming a single actor with a single defense and foreign policy, it will in essence become a new, much larger state. The European Monetary Union is a step in this direction but is in itself insufficient.

But on the way to paramountcy as a manner of organization, the nation-state underwent an odd metamorphosis. First, internal sovereignty declined such that it was shared more broadly within the state as the individual and groups obtained "representation." In many cases, internal sovereignty became reallocated across regions and levels of government through federalism, thus taking the rough edges off power distribution as well.[28]

Second, external sovereignty has declined, although not as rapidly and extensively as internal sovereignty. Interdependence between countries of approximately equal size and countries geographically contiguous and culturally similar is now commonplace. Interdependence not only implies cooperation and a comparative absence of power politics. It also implies involuntary participation in management of common problems, such as the effort to contain inflation, or to stem unemployment, or to deter a mutual threat. Alone this management is impossible, but together otherwise sovereign and separate governments can concert an effective policy. Interdependence has not replaced power politics, but power politics must share its role with interdependence. Military power is still the arbiter of the nation-state. Interdependence in some places and on some issues is now of consequence in the portfolio of foreign policy interaction.

Two noteworthy principles emerge from this analysis:

- As external sovereignty has declined historically, the integrity of the nation-state has nonetheless increased. This is peculiar in the sense that the opposite might have been expected. The decline in sovereignty might have been expected to lead to erosion of security and the collapse of government. That this has not happened is directly the result of the changes in the military behavior of states discussed earlier in this chapter. Security of the nation-state is now more permanent and less subject to perpetual test than ever before, although the ultimate threat of society-destroying war is ever present. The probability of a loss of territorial sovereignty has declined even as the potential cost of all-out war has soared.

- As internal sovereignty has declined, the cause of individual freedom has improved. This development, too, is not intuitive: the decline of internal sovereignty has meant that the individual has found more effective political representation. The Leviathan has not descended into civil war even as its superstructure has been dismantled somewhat and its responsibilities are shared more broadly from within. Indeed, one could argue that the decline of internal sovereignty was essential to the better provision of safeguards to the freedom of the individual citizen.

What we see in the NAFTA context is a playing out of each of these principles. A reduction of the barriers established to defend external sovereignty has neither threatened the three peoples—the Mexican, the American, the Canadian—nor weakened their governments. Greater wealth has created a stronger economic and power base for each state. Canada in the short term may question this in the face of Quebec separation, but the per capita wealth of the society continues to grow. Quebec cohesion has not suffered from a decline of external sovereignty. Nor would Canadian unity have benefited from the lessened prosperity accompanying high tariff walls. If Canada breaks up, the burden cannot be placed on the shoulders of NAFTA. The best test of the latter proposition concerning individual freedom is the Mexican case in which greater openness and increased propensity for democracy go hand in hand with the emergence of a freedom-minded middle class.

Conclusion

In sum, political sovereignty has two faces, an internal face and an external face.[29] Despite the high value placed on both types of sovereignty, each has declined in magnitude over recent centuries with spectacular consequence for the nation-state. Yet the nation-state shows no prospect of disappearing. Nor does the multinational firm appear likely to assume the sovereignty of the nation-state, regardless of how much financial and commercial control technology seems to have shifted to the firm. Sovereignty reduction seems to have approached asymptotes of constraint that will reinforce the autonomy of the nation-state into the twenty-first century.[30] In North America, NAFTA will deepen and it will widen. But the strategy of integration is likely to be pragmatic and piecemeal. Perhaps this strategy is one of the things that unite all North Americans.

Hence, despite the reality that sovereignty is thought to be a kind of Platonic good in itself, the relaxation of sovereignty has yielded unexpected benefits. There are limits, however, as to how far such relaxation can go both internally and externally. The modern democracy, and liberal state, has probably explored and reached those limits. Without a further set of innovations led by technology, the modern nation-state cannot devolve sovereignty much beyond the present asymptote and still continue to exist as it is politically now constituted.

Notes

1. Charles F. Doran, "Trade Dispute Resolution 'On Trial': Softwood Lumber," *International Journal* 51 (Autumn 1996): 709–733. See also Charles F. Doran and Timothy J. Naftali, *U.S.-Canadian Softwood Lumber: Trade Dispute Negotiations*, Foreign Policy Institute Case Studies No. 8 (Washington, D.C.: Johns Hopkins University, 1987).

2. Canadian critics described CUFTA as a time-bomb because it did not resolve the question of subsidies and countervailing duties with finality before signature of the arrangement. Robert Bothwell, *Canada and the United States* (New York: Twayne Publishers, 1992), 148.

3. Canadian managers still often see "rationalization" as a threat to their jobs as Canadian units are incorporated into larger "North American units." Defensiveness extends to fear of becoming not a branch plant but a fully incorporated subunit of a U.S.-based multinational enterprise. See "U.S. Firms in North America: Redefining Structure and Strategy," *North American Outlook* 5, no. 2 (February 1995): 58.

4. Substitution of procurement requirements and anticompetition practice for subsidies, for instance, must next be addressed in a climate virtually free of formal tariffs. Peter Morici, *Free Trade in the Americas* (New York: Twentieth Century Fund / Inter-American Dialogue Monograph, 1994), 14.

5. In A. Michael Spence and Heather A. Hazard, *International Competitiveness* (Cambridge: Ballinger, 1988), xxi.

6. Hiroshi Okumura, "The Closed Nature of Japanese Intercorporate Relations," *Japan Echo* 9, no. 3 (1982): 59–61.

7. Charles F. Doran, *Systems in Crisis* (Cambridge: Cambridge University Press, 1991).

8. Coproduction via the *maquiladora* plants, for example, becomes thinkable despite pressure from organized labor. Sidney Weintraub, "Global Corporations and Developing Countries," in *Global Corporations and Nation-states: Do Companies or Countries Compete?* ed. Richard S. Belous and Kelly L. McClenahan, (Washington, D.C.: National Planning Association, 1991), 72.

9. Chalmers Johnson notes, for example, the Japanese distinction between formal sovereignty, *tatemae*, and the hegemony of a covert elite working group, *honne*, that is actually in charge. Such a distinction is important to Japan and to a number of other countries like Germany and South Korea and takes the predominant Western meaning of sovereignty in quite a different direction. "The State and Japanese Grand Strategy," in *The Domestic Bases of Grand Strategy*, ed. Richard Rosecrance and Arthur A. Stein (Ithaca, N.Y.: Cornell University Press, 1993), 221.

10. Robert Keohane notes that sovereignty "refers to a legal status," and that it does not imply "defacto independence." He rejects Waltz's use of the term sovereignty as "deciding for itself" what its own behavior will be. But Keohane then goes on to consider sovereignty as a "practice" in Rawls's sense of rule-defined behavior. Of course sovereignty can be regarded merely as an international legal concept depicting only legal status, but that is not the sense that is most helpful in world politics. In practice, sovereignty does imply both rule-based and behavioral considerations, that is, in the end, political independence. *International Institutions and State Power* (Boulder, Colo.: Westview Press, 1989), 165.

11. Michael Nicholson argues that "repression" of unwanted political and social behavior (the Freudian id) is necessary at the individual level if cooperation is to flourish. He sees this repression as a substitute for that of Hobbes's Sovereign who repressed the "collective ego." Yet, in each case, is "repression" the correct strategy? The analytic task is to find alternate strategies to repression or suppression. That is the brilliance of the democratic initiative. *Rationality and the Analysis of International Conflict* (Cambridge: Cambridge University Press, 1992), 114.

12. Niccolo Machiavelli, *The Prince*, trans. Luigi Ricci (Chicago: Oxford University Press, The Great Books Foundation, 1955), chap. 15, p. 51.

13. Reinhold Niebuhr, *Moral Man and Immoral Society* (New York: Charles Scribner's Sons, 1932), 1960.

14. Roger Chauvire, *Jean Bodin, auteur de la republique* (Paris, 1914), and *Jean Bodin: Sechs Bücher über den Staat*, trans. von Bernd Wimmer (Munich: C.H. Beck., 1981).

15. Dorothy Whitelock, *The Beginnings of English Society* (Harmondsworth: Penguin Books, 1952), 30–31.

16. George E. G. Catlin, *Thomas Hobbes as Philosopher, Publicist, and Man of Letters* (Oxford: Oxford University Press, 1922).

17. T. B. Bottomore, *Elites and Society* (Harmondsworth: Penguin Books, 1964), 112–128; Gaetano Mosca, *The Ruling Class* (New York: McGraw-Hill, 1939), especially 413–419.

18. See for example the symposium on federalism in *PS: Political Science and Politics*, June 1993, especially John Kincaid, "Constitutional Federal-

ism," 172–177; and Beverly A. Cigler, "Challenges Facing Fiscal Federalism in the 1990s," 181–186. John A. McDougall, "North American Integration and Canadian Disunity," *Canadian Public Policy* 17, no. 4 (1991): 395–408; Jean-Luc Migue, "Retour du vrai federalisme, institutionalization de la concurrence entre gouvernements," in *Document de travail, numero 4* (Belanger Campeau Commission sur l'Avenir Politique et Constitutionnel du Quebec), 681–719; Jorge G. Castaneda, "Can NAFTA Change Mexico?" *Foreign Affairs* 72, no. 4 (1993): 66–80.

19. James Mayall reminds us that any limitations on sovereignty must be "voluntarily agreed." This is a cornerstone of modern international law. Equality before the law is one of the assumptions that preface limitation. *Nationalism and International Society* (Cambridge: Cambridge University Press, 1991), 37.

20. "The pursuit of order . . . has reinforced the hierarchical dimensions of international society since the powerful states are, by definition, best placed to resist any change which adversely affects their interests." In Ian Clark, *The Hierarchy of States* (Cambridge: Cambridge University Press, 1989), 30.

21. In a book whose lessons have been too much neglected, Zbigniew Brzezinski provides a ledger of the human cost of communism in the twentieth century. He estimates, conservatively, 50 million fatalities. *The Grand Failure: The Birth and Death of Communism in the Twentieth Century* (New York: Charles Scribner's Sons, 1989), 239–240.

22. Peter Drucker, *Post-Capitalist Society* (New York: HarperCollins, 1993), 164.

23. Eastern Europe and Asia did not provide the basis of "negotiation" among groups and classes observed in Western Europe and hence slipped into despotism. John Breuilly, *Nationalism and the State*, 2d ed. (Chicago: University of Chicago Press, 1994), 374.

24. Simon Kuznets observes that authoritarian society (in which internal sovereignty is presumably maximized) acts as a "backward" society in which the society is not concerned with new invention but only with imitation and the drawing down of past discovery by others. *Toward a Theory of Economic Growth* (New York: Norton, 1968), 73.

25. For one interpretation of this message, drawing upon contemporary economic theory of innovation and empirical analysis, see Kristian Palda, *Innovation Policy and Canada's Competitiveness* (Vancouver, British Columbia: The Fraser Institute, 1993).

26. According to one interpretation, only with the advent of the absolutist state were the rising middle classes able to put their trust in the Crown. It was then that the feudal dominance of the aristocracy that had ruled since the fall of the Roman Empire was put to an end. A. R. Myers, *England in the Late Middle Ages* (Harmondsworth: Penguin Books, 1952), 21–22.

27. Consider, for example, W. J. Eccles, *France in America*, rev. ed. (1972; revised, Markham: Fitzhenry & Whiteside, 1990), 63–95.

28. Here I tend to agree with my colleague, Christoph Schreuer, who argues that "rather than grope for the seat of sovereignty, we should adjust

our intellectual framework to a multi-layered reality consisting of a variety of authoritative structures." In "The Waning of the Sovereign State: Towards a New Paradigm for International Law?" *European Journal of International Law* 4, no. 4 (1993): 453.

29. To place this interpretation in the context of the present debate over sovereignty, consider the excellent analysis of the political science literature in Janice E. Thompson, "State Sovereignty in International Relations: Bridging the Gap Between Theory and Empirical Research," *International Studies Quarterly* 39, no. 2 (June 1995): 213–236.

30. Kant warned of these internal and external constraints (i.e., a "harmony to emerge among men through their discord") amounting to no less than a conception of the balance of power among sovereign entities. Immanuel Kant, *Perpetual Peace and Other Essays* (1795; reprint, Indianapolis: Hackett, 1983), 120. According to F. H. Hinsley, however, "a sovereign authority may subscribe to such limitations as follow from it without ceasing to be sovereign." But how far can this go politically before a state ceases to be a state? *Sovereignty*, 2d ed. (Cambridge: Cambridge University Press, 1986), 232.

6

NAFTA and U.S. Economic Sovereignty

Sidney Weintraub

Then along comes the International Trade Organization with the 58 nations, as I have already explained, with 58 votes. We shall have the same vote as Lithuania, Siam, and the smallest nations of the world, so we shall have 1 vote to their 57.
—Senator George Wilson Malone (R-Nev.),
Congressional Record, March 31, 1949[1]

The core procedural rule of trade policy is secrecy.
—Ralph Nader, "Introduction: Free Trade and
the Decline of Democracy," in *The Case
Against Free Trade*, 1993[2]

NAFTA is about a New World Order; . . . it is about a loss of American sovereignty.
—Pat Buchanan, *Washington Times*, September 22, 1993

Schizophrenia about national roles in the world economy is a common ailment from which the United States is not immune. The United States took the lead in negotiating the International Trade Organization (ITO), the so-called Havana Charter, at the end of World War II out of a desire to free world trade from the nationalistic restrictions that had prevailed in the interwar period. That creation was killed at birth out of fear that it would lead to too much meddling in U.S. trade decisions. This double vision—the conflict between opening the markets of others while maintaining U.S. freedom of action with respect to its own market—reappeared in 1994 when the World Trade Organization (WTO) was put forward for congressional approval, but this time the WTO was approved.[3] The main arguments against the ITO and the WTO were eerily identical, although 45 years apart; namely, that the United States would be outvoted in a crunch.

Some of this sentiment—that Canada and Mexico would gang up against the United States—was present in the opposition to the North American Free Trade Agreement (NAFTA), but the main sovereignty arguments were different in that case. One form they took was that as "environmental and safety standards are 'harmonized' (made the same everywhere) . . . the practical result [would be] that they would be pulled down toward a lowest common denominator level."[4] One could substitute the words "labor standards" or "wages" or "sanitary regulations" for environmental and safety standards; the thesis is that the United States would lose its sovereign independence to deal with key economic and related matters.

Then, a year later in early 1995, the opposition to providing a $40 billion loan guarantee to enable Mexico to roll over its short-term debt ran into fierce opposition in the U.S. Congress on essentially the same populist-nationalist grounds. When it appeared that the legislation would be defeated, despite support from the leadership of both U.S. political parties, Pat Buchanan wrote in evident exultation: "Economic nationalism has just scored a stunning upset."[5] President Clinton, because of this opposition, provided the support to Mexico by executive action together with large international contributions from the International Monetary Fund (IMF) and the Bank for International Settlements (BIS).

When the NAFTA process started, the expectation of experts on Mexico was that sovereign sensitivity would be greatest there because of the country's historical experience of invasion and economic pressure from the United States. The step toward free trade was a profound policy shift for Mexico, which traditionally had conducted its affairs to distance itself as much as possible from its powerful northern neighbor. Sovereign sensitivity was not expected to be as significant in the United States. This was a miscalculation. The Mexican population took the change in the economic relationship more or less in stride—at least until Mexico's economic collapse in 1995—whereas the U.S. population did not.[6]

There is a bigger issue at play here than just U.S.-Mexico relations. Ambivalence over the growing U.S. involvement in global economic affairs remains a major feature of the U.S. political scene. U.S. exports of goods and services now constitute 10 percent of gross domestic product (GDP), but there is still much railing over competitive imports.[7] NAFTA was sold to the general public on the basis that it promoted U.S. exports, hence U.S.

jobs, and scant regard was given to the two-way nature of trade. Mercantilism is alive and well in the United States.

The growth of U.S. foreign direct investment (FDI) exceeds the growth of exports, and this gives rise to perennial complaints about the loss of U.S. jobs.[8] This contention was the essence of Ross Perot's "giant sucking sound." The fact that U.S. exports follow U.S. FDI is generally ignored. The United States relies on substantial inflows of foreign capital to augment national savings and to finance the current account deficit in the U.S. balance of payments, yet there is a gut populist sentiment to isolate the United States from the effects of international capital flows. This was evident in the Mexico peso guarantee debate.[9]

The discussion that follows deals first with the reasons for the broad misgivings about the growing U.S. economic involvement in the world economy—to ask the question of what brings on the populist resentment that is evident on both the left and the right of U.S. society. The second major part of the chapter looks more precisely at sovereignty hang-ups as they emerged in specific cases, such as the opposition to NAFTA and then the peso support program for Mexico.

The Diminution of Sovereignty

The economic sovereignty dilemma of the United States—and of any country that is not an autarky—begins when international trade takes place. Blame Adam Smith or David Ricardo for showing that nations increase their welfare from international trade. The dilemma is stated simply and well in an article by Conrad Weiler: "The more we demand rules of fair and free world trade, the more we will become subject to those rules."[10]

This citation refers to trade, but the dilemma is deeper than this. It extends as well to capital flows, environmental protection, dealing with narcotics traffic, and upgrading the treatment of labor. The battlefields are often multinational institutions, like the IMF, that impose economic conditions on countries seeking assistance, and the United Nations itself, which levies charges on countries for all kinds of operations from peacekeeping and peacemaking to technical assistance in a variety of fields.

The dilemma is particularly acute in a federal system in which the component units—the states in the United States, the provinces in Canada, and (increasingly) the states in Mexico—have considerable sovereign power of their own. This issue arose in the General Agreement on Tariffs and Trade (GATT), subsequently in the Canada-U.S. Free Trade Agreement (CUFTA), and then in NAFTA. The challenges to the sovereignty of subunits of nations rest largely on a perennial provision of international trade agreements that standards of various kinds and taxes must apply equally to like national and foreign products—and this in a federal system necessarily affects states and provinces as well as national governments.[11] The NAFTA implementing legislation in the United States seeks to deal with this through a federal-state consultation process to identify inconsistencies between state laws and NAFTA provisions and the potential for grandfathering pre-existing state laws. This is not necessarily a solution to the problem but rather provides for an ongoing process to deal with the issue as cases arise.

The compromising of national sovereignties only increased as transportation and communication technologies improved. Moving goods from place to place became cheaper and swifter. Following the logic of the early theorists, efficient transportation technology could provide nations with augmented welfare gains from trade. The accelerated communications advances that the world is now experiencing permit instantaneous transmission of information and the transfer of funds across national borders in the time it takes to give a computer command.

When the IMF was created after World War II, there was concern that the capital flows that then existed could overwhelm national monetary and economic policy. Indeed, the articles of the IMF even encouraged nations to limit flows of capital as opposed to current transactions. This now seems quaint some 50 years later when these flows exceed $1 trillion every working day. Germany could not resist upward valuation of its currency in the early 1970s because of what was then considered the massive inflow of billions of dollars a day betting on appreciation of the deutsche mark. Chile, in 1994, was forced to appreciate its currency because of modest capital inflows, which it resisted. In the case of Mexico at the end of 1994, the devaluation of the peso was caused by growing capital flight leading to a dangerous loss of reserves.

Under modern circumstances, there is no way to achieve complete independence of domestic monetary policy—unless the nation is a hermit dictatorship. North Korea and Myanmar have more economic sovereignty than do the United States and South Korea, but at an enormous price. During 1994, the U.S. Federal Reserve Board raised interest rates repeatedly. The fallout was not confined to the domestic market but had substantial repercussions on our NAFTA partners. The already high interest cost of Canada's budget went even higher, and Mexico was forced to raise its interest rates to attract portfolio capital.

Modern world production and marketing techniques have increasingly made earlier notions of sovereignty—controlling what is made at home and what is sold at home—antiquated. Large corporations of all nationalities scan the globe for production possibilities. It is an increasing trend that trade in intermediate products takes place between related firms, such as an engine produced in Mexico for incorporation in a car assembled in the United States. The majority of trade in manufactured goods between the United States and its two NAFTA partners is of this nature—intrafirm or between related firms.[12] It is well nigh impossible for the purchaser of a final product to know what components came from which countries.

Can this trend be reversed, which would be necessary to reclaim the old-fashioned sovereignty of "Buy American" or that of whatever country is named? The short answer is no, unless the United States is prepared to close in on itself and not participate in what has become a worldwide practice. The clamor by the AFL-CIO against the *maquiladora* production in Mexico—under which component parts are sent to Mexico for further elaboration and reshipment of the product, including the non-U.S. value added, back to the United States—is based on a desire to turn off this process. Ralph Nader made the suggestion that when corporations go abroad in this way, the resulting elaborated product should be refused entry into the United States.[13] What would then happen to Mexico's capacity to purchase from the United States goods and services, which are also produced or generated by U.S. workers?[14] What would happen to U.S. exports to developing countries generally—and they are the fastest-growing U.S. foreign markets—if they were denied the employment-generating and export-earning capacity of coproduction?

The philosophic transformation that has taken place in Latin America since the early to mid-1980s has put even more pressure on old-fashioned sovereigntists. The dominant development model in Latin America until then was to foster domestic industry protected by high barriers against imports and to reject FDI as diluting national control over a country's economy. This type of industrialization was seen by its Mexican proponents as a way to reduce U.S. influence.[15] The model broke down during the debt crisis of the 1980s when it became evident that economic isolation of this nature did precious little to protect sovereignty if a country could not meet its foreign obligations.

The development model that now prevails in most of Latin America is to open import markets and to seek out FDI as a way to stimulate exports and thereby generate economic growth. The economic success of the Asian tigers and of Chile in the Western Hemisphere using a policy of promoting exports had a powerful influence on the slower-growing, debt-ridden countries of the Western Hemisphere. This policy is often referred to as economic neoliberalism, using the word *liberal* by way of harking back to the early trade policy theorists.[16]

The shift in development philosophy was a rejection of the earlier conception that economic sovereignty required closed markets and the adoption of a more expansive version of sovereignty, one that required cooperatively open markets.

This new conception of sovereignty stimulated economic regionalism of a very different variety from what had existed earlier. The 1950s and 1960s version of economic integration in Latin America sought essentially to expand the scope of import substitution to a larger area—to all of Latin America, for example, in the Latin American Free Trade Association (LAFTA). But LAFTA collapsed. The dominant current form of economic integration is called open integration precisely to differentiate it from the earlier closed version that demanded high import barriers against the outside world.[17]

The breakdown of the old version was the result of unequal benefits among the member countries.[18] The more developed among them, such as Argentina, Brazil, and Mexico, obtained the major benefits while the least developed found themselves paying higher prices for goods that earlier could be imported from nonmember countries. This was a classic illustration for the least-developed countries in the hemisphere of trade-diverting integration. The current version does not repeat the critical fault of the earlier model of forcing high import barriers on the weaker countries. It remains to be seen whether open regionalism is more successful than the former closed version, but it certainly represents a major shift in how economic sovereignty is viewed.

The shift in thinking in the hemisphere, from protecting relatively closed markets to emphasizing export expansion—from import substitution to economic neoliberalism—puts into sharp focus the debate over sovereignty in the United States. It is not only Mexico that requires an open U.S. market to achieve its long-term development objectives; it is most of the countries of the Western Hemisphere. During the 10 years from 1985 to 1994, U.S. merchandise exports to Latin America grew by 200 percent (in nominal dollars). They grew by a like percentage to Asia, excluding Japan. These two regions were the fastest growing for U.S. exports. This export growth could not have been accomplished had the U.S. market not also been relatively open to imports from them.

U.S. policy must confront in this hemisphere, as it did earlier in Asia, that the centerpiece of relations is now trade and investment. When the United States succeeded in getting hemispheric countries to shift from expecting aid to relying on trade to drive development policy, there was an inevitable loss of U.S. economic sovereignty. Aid is given unilaterally; trade requires negotiation and reciprocity.

Now that the central aspiration of the countries of the hemisphere—achieving high rates of economic growth—is intimately related to export expansion, the United States would have nothing to say to them if it reverted to nationalistic protectionism. This became evident at the Summit of the Americas held in Miami in early December 1994. The United States first suggested a formless agenda that gave trade issues an equal place with matters of governance (democracy) and sustainable development (that is, a focus on environmental issues). The other countries of the hemisphere insisted that trade be given higher priority; in effect, that there was little to be said about the other issues in the absence of a trade focus.

These issues of complex interdependence—what should remain as national prerogatives and how these prerogatives must be tempered—are near ubiquitous. Human rights abuses in individual countries can no longer be defended on sovereignty grounds. Countries cannot rely on the sovereignty defense when they pollute the environment. There is no such thing as a purely national defense against narcotics traffic. Internet is rapidly destroying the ability of governments to close off their national territories to information from the outside.

Canada and Mexico, the two U.S. partners in NAFTA, have long recognized that their monetary independence is compromised by their reliance on the U.S. capital market. Both Mexico and Canada would have preferred lower interest rates in 1994 to deal with their fiscal problems, but this was impossible in any practical sense after U.S. interest rates started to rise. The United States felt more insulated from developments in its two neighbors because of its greater economic power, but it then learned that sovereignty was no defense against a financial meltdown in Mexico. The United States also learned that when the Mexican currency is under attack—when U.S. exports to Mexico must fall as Mexico goes through economic restructuring—the dollar also can come under attack.

The Mexican financial crisis is stimulating a debate about the future role of the IMF. The IMF contributed $17.8 billion to the Mexican rescue package, the largest such contribution in its history. The funds were patched together under the pressure of crisis. The rationale for the assistance was that if the Mexican meltdown were not contained, the repercussions would upset financial markets across the globe. This may or may not have been the correct judgment, but the dual questions of avoiding such meltdowns and enlarging the resources of the IMF to enable it to meet comparable emergencies in the future without going through the contortions it faced this time have been on the table ever since.[19]

It has long been second nature to those engaged in international economic matters that no precise line could be drawn separating national from international affairs. This is more true today than ever before as capital flows have skyrocketed and trade flows continue to rise. Multinational firms cannot be turned inward. Information flows cannot be stanched. Even people cannot be kept out if they are determined to emigrate from one place to another. These are all areas in which undesirable outcomes can perhaps be mitigated—for example, slowing down the inflow of volatile capital or of unwanted immigrants—but only if there is cooperation among countries. And once the need for cooperation is admitted, so too is it evident that sovereignty is not a purely national choice in many of the most important aspects of the international economy.

The North American Context

The NAFTA debate brought out many U.S. hang-ups over sovereignty—about U.S. control over developments within its own borders—that were lurking just below the surface in connection with U.S. participation in the GATT. These concerns became more explicit in the NAFTA context. For example,

- *the movement of production outside the United States.* This has been taking place for some time, but the issue was highlighted by the prospect of free trade with a neighboring low-wage country.

- *the establishment of trinational commissions to monitor enforcement of labor and environmental laws.* The two supplemental agreements on these issues heightened this concern because they also entailed potential trade penalties to be decided by the commissions. The U.S. Trade Representative took great pains to reject the suggestion that there was any intention of "fashioning supplemental agreements that intruded on our sovereignty."[20]

- *the lack of explicit provisions in NAFTA for dealing with environmental concerns arising from the processes used in the production of goods,* as opposed to sanitary problems related to the goods themselves. This arose from the decision by a GATT panel in a 1991 ruling against U.S. import restrictions, under the Marine Mammal Protection Act, on tuna from Mexico caught by methods that resulted in excessive dolphin kills.

- *the concern that the dispute-settlement procedure for dealing with antidumping and countervailing duty issues, as embodied in chapter 19 of NAFTA, removes these issues from U.S. courts and places them instead in the hands of panelists from the two disputing countries.* This provision of NAFTA was based on a similar provision in CUFTA.[21]

The question of how deeply the existence of NAFTA involved the joint sovereignties of the member countries was brought out with particular force in the financial rescue package following the Mexican peso devaluation. Rightly or wrongly, the U.S. Treasury, supported by the chairman of the Federal Reserve Board, concluded that a Mexican default on its short-term obligations would have serious adverse effects on the international financial system as a whole. The loan package was designed to prevent this outcome.

The U.S. loan enabled Mexico to avoid default on its dollar obligations.[22] Two things are clear, however. The first is that the Mexican authorities felt they had no choice but to accept onerous economic conditions imposed from the outside, by the IMF and the U.S. government, that were highly unpopular politically.[23] The United States, for its part, felt obliged to come to the rescue of Mexico despite the opposition evident among the general public and members of Congress from both parties. The responsible authorities on each side rejected the more popular invocation of national sovereignty to kill the loan package and its conditions.

Was this decision by both parties propelled by the existence of NAFTA? Probably, in part. Had the rescue package not been forthcoming, it is likely that Mexico would have been forced to impose capital controls because of the inability to roll over its debt at an acceptable cost. Restrictions on imports from the United States might have been instituted as a way to quickly reduce the current account deficit. Either action, especially the latter, could have destroyed NAFTA.[24]

But it is important to remember that this was not the first U.S. economic rescue package for Mexico. There were loans in 1982, when Mexico was forced to seek rescheduling of its debt; and there was debt restructuring several times during the 1980s. In the ordering of the U.S. foreign policy interests in Mexico, the highest priority has long been the maintenance of stability there. The main stated reason for the 1995 rescue package was to prevent disturbances in the international financial system. Although not given as much prominence in official statements, an equally important motive was to limit instability in Mexico that would propel a wave of undocumented immigration.

The U.S. government has taken pains to state that the Mexican rescue should not be viewed as a precedent of action that would be taken if other countries found themselves in similar straits.[25] Mexico is a neighbor and that imposes limits on the freedom of action of each country.

There was some disconnect in the debate on NAFTA itself in that its proponents stressed the welfare benefits that would accrue to all three countries from more open markets, while its opponents emphasized the diminution in national decision-making. This was the nature of the debate in Canada in the national election in 1988 that preceded the entry into force of CUFTA. The sovereignty issue did not loom large in the United States in the Canadian case. But it did when the free-trade partner was Mexico. For those who watched both debates, there was a peculiar transference under which many in the United States reacted toward Mexico in much the same way that Canadian opponents of CUFTA had reacted toward the United States.

The issue in the NAFTA debate, at its core, was welfare versus sovereignty. This overstates, perhaps, because NAFTA opponents also disputed the welfare gains from free trade with Mexico, but there were few competent analysts to make a convincing case on this. U.S. economists in overwhelming proportion supported NAFTA. Opposition to NAFTA focused on maintaining the unilateral right to keep out low-wage Mexican goods and limiting the movement of production to Mexico. There was fear that NAFTA would result in the forced adoption by the United States of the lowest common denominator environmental standards and practices—those of Mexico.[26]

The sovereignty issue also had much to do with choosing the form of North American economic integration. Canadians made clear their preference—insistence is probably the better word—for the free-trade area (FTA) form of integration rather than a customs union (CU). Under an FTA, each country can maintain its own external tariff toward nonmembers, whereas under a CU there is a common external tariff (CET). Perhaps even more significant, a CU involves a common commercial policy; more significant because even in an FTA there is a tendency for tariff levels to equalize for intermediate and capital goods, else the country with the lower tariffs would be a favored location for investment. What Canada seemed to fear most was that it might be pressured to adopt many restrictive U.S. commercial measures, such as embargoes against Cuba and Vietnam or restrictions on subsidiaries of Canadian corporations in their business dealings with Cuba.

Whether these concerns were justified or not, a CU clearly implied one further degree of integration—one further bit of diminution of economic sovereignty—than was necessary in an FTA. The Mexicans felt the same way and were therefore quite content with the FTA form of economic integration. So too, really, was the United States. All three chose this form despite its major shortcoming of requiring detailed rules of origin to prevent transshipment of goods imported first into the lower tariff country but destined for the higher tariff country. This technical issue need not arise in a CU because the external tariff is the same.

When the question of economic integration first arose, some critics argued that a major shortcoming was that while it would in due course permit the free movement of goods and most services, and of capital, there was no provision for the free movement of labor. The European Common Market, today's

European Union (EU), does call for free labor movement among the member countries. Yet, the idea of a North American common market was a nonstarter other than as a rhetorical gambit. When Mexicans called for free labor movement, they had in mind mostly low-skilled workers, which was precisely what the United States would not accept. It is unlikely that either Canada or Mexico would have permitted the free movement of skilled labor from the United States.

An FTA was chosen over a CU precisely because it called for less sacrifice of sovereignty. A common market was rejected out of hand by the United States because it would entail loss of U.S. choice over who could enter the country. North America has greater limits than Western Europe on the degree to which the countries are willing to forgo sovereign choices. Despite the unwillingness of the United States to formally accept the free movement of labor in North America, there is in fact more labor movement from Mexico to the United States than there is among countries of the EU. The labor flows from Mexico are a mixture of the legal and undocumented, but the people come regardless of the formal arrangements.

For the time being, in 1996, the preoccupation in North America is largely the financial-economic recovery in Mexico following the sharp decline of 6.9 percent in GDP in 1995. Trade flows between Mexico and the United States altered drastically as the result of the austerity measures imposed to restore economic confidence and the large peso devaluation of about 50 percent. Mexico had a large current account deficit in 1994; this was largely eliminated in 1995. Nevertheless, Mexico will one day come out of its present economic turmoil, and the rationale for economic integration in North America will reassert itself. In the interim, NAFTA itself will likely deepen although perhaps at a pace slower than earlier contemplated.

The coproduction that exists surely will continue. It even accelerated during the Mexican adjustment in 1995 because of the abnormally low wage rates that prevailed. In the immediate aftermath of the peso meltdown, the Mexican authorities went beyond the strict provisions of NAFTA and opened the country's financial sector—particularly banking—to attract more foreign participation. Customs clearance is still inefficient, and work will continue to move goods more efficiently and expeditiously between NAFTA countries to permit just-in-time production methods. Product standards must be agreed to optimize coproduction, to assure that an intermediate product produced in one country can be used in assembling products in the other two. NAFTA, in the year 2000, will provide that trucks from the member countries can move from one end of North America to the other, and rules must be worked out for safety and emissions standards. The dispute settlement arrangements must still be refined. Talks are taking place on devising better procedures for dealing with charges of dumping and subsidies.

NAFTA cannot stand still as barriers to trade and investment, to transportation and communication, come down. And as NAFTA deepens in these fields, old habits of sovereignty will have to give way. Truckers, if the borders are in fact opened, will think in North American terms. As Mexico's national railway is privatized, the rail systems of the three countries will become more integrated. The ability of national governments to use product standards as a protective device will diminish.

The area that may become the most contentious is dealing with exchange rate policy and balance-of-payments issues. The result of what turned out to be faulty policy in this field is not only tragedy for the Mexican population but also stimulation for the involvement of the United States and the injection of a vast sum of money. Mexico had insisted on its right to pursue its own policy, but the cost of its errors did not respect the border. It is unclear where the Mexican peso will settle when the financial situation works its way out of crisis, but the substantial depreciation with respect to the dollar will drastically alter trade patterns for a number of years. The average Mexican tariff is about 11 percent, but the exchange rate depreciation is around 50 percent. NAFTA deals with the lesser of these two determinants of trade.

This area—dealing with exchange rates and balance-of-payments considerations—will inevitably be brought under closer scrutiny in the context of NAFTA. This is already taking place because of the conditions the United States is imposing on its $20 billion loan plus the incorporation of IMF conditions dealing with monetary and fiscal policy. The form that this exchange rate consultation will take as the emergency passes cannot be specified now, but neither can the problem be ignored.

Economic sovereignty used to consist of the ability to specify the levels of national tariff and nontariff barriers. This was gradually undermined by negotiations in the GATT and even more by the conclusion of NAFTA. Determining national monetary and fiscal policy is perhaps the ultimate manifestation of economic sovereignty. Mexico lost control over this aspect of its national prerogative when it obtained massive outside help to overcome its economic emergency. This is not a new phenomenon in that access to IMF resources has always involved conditions dealing with national macroeconomic policy. But NAFTA may require close monitoring in this field even in the absence of an emergency.

The meaning of sovereignty has long been nebulous for the issues of this discussion. Being next to a dominant economic power has meant that neither Canada nor Mexico could have a completely national monetary policy. Neither could run protracted fiscal deficits without some impact on their credit ratings when borrowing in the U.S. and international capital markets.

The United States discovered long ago that having a poor, low-wage country next door limited its control over who enters the country. There is much rhetoric about regaining control over the U.S. border, but the truth is that this control never really existed. This became evident in 1995 as Mexican incomes declined and incentives to emigrate to the United States rose. The U.S. response has been to beef up surveillance at the border to stanch this flow.

Narcotics cross borders. So do air and water pollution. Information cannot be bottled up in this age of cyberspace. Volatile capital flows can perhaps be slowed somewhat but not completely. Mexico learned this when the banks were nationalized in 1982—capital still fled Mexico because there was a rational motive for getting one's money out.

These conditions antedate NAFTA. NAFTA, however, intensifies their effect.

Conclusions

Other than extremists on both the left and the right, there is general recognition among informed observers of U.S. participation in the international economy that some sovereignty is sacrificed in exchange for benefits from other countries. Sovereignty in this definition refers to national control over decisions affecting the national economy. Much of this diminution of sovereignty is routine: tariffs are bound in GATT negotiations in exchange for reciprocal bindings; international codes of conduct on foreign investment are accepted; environmental protection is agreed internationally; resolutions on working conditions and child labor are agreed in the International Labor Organization (ILO). The International Convention on Human Rights is perhaps the best example in the social field of the principle that domestic actions are subject to international scrutiny.

The majority of complaints in this field arise not because of sovereignty diminution but instead because "other" countries are not living up to commitments made. The slogan that the United States wants fair trade is typical of this genre of objection to further opening the U.S. market to imports. What these complaints make clear is that while sovereignty is diminished, it is not given up. Countries can raise bound tariffs, but in principle they must compensate other countries when this is done. Despite ILO conventions, sweatshops exist throughout the world. Not all countries are scrupulous in protecting human rights, but the international convention does prescribe a goal, a limit, that the international community hopes to attain. The existence of such commitments, whether economic or social, makes breaches of their terms a legitimate subject for international criticism.

NAFTA, whose objective is to integrate the three economies of North America, takes these long-standing international practices one step further. Most tariff and nontariff barriers will be eliminated, not just reduced, in trade among the member countries. Investment within the region is largely free of prior screening. Disputes over the imposition of countervailing and antidumping duties can be appealed to binational panels instead of national courts. The parallel agreements on labor and the environment permit the imposition of limited trade penalties when an international commission concludes that the agreements have been violated.

Once again, however, the national power to make decisions in these fields is not removed by NAFTA. A country can be penalized when its decisions contravene agreed understandings, but even this is constrained. As with GATT undertakings, countries enter into these agreements because the obligations undertaken are balanced by benefits received in reciprocal negotiations.

Just as international trade and investment developments have successively reduced the scope for national action, so too will the existence of NAFTA. In order for NAFTA to maximize benefits—efficient production, regional marketing, unencumbered investment, swift resolution of disputes, greater protection of intellectual property, and many other advantages—it must deepen beyond its current status. This has been the history of trade opening generally. The limit in the economic field is economic and monetary union, the goal of the EU, but there is no contemplation that NAFTA will go that far. The very choice of the FTA rather than a CU or common market form is an indication of the more limited NAFTA objective. But NAFTA almost certainly will get into areas such as dealing with exchange rate relationships that are not now part of the agreement.

NAFTA is different from the EU in another important respect: the existence in NAFTA of a powerful country, a middle power, and a developing country. The EU has several near equals—Germany, France, the United Kingdom, Italy. Thus the dependency in NAFTA is more asymmetrical than in the EU. The United States is affected by monetary and fiscal policy in Canada and Mexico, as is evident from Mexico's financial crisis and the low level of the Canadian dollar with respect to the U.S. dollar, but much less than the reverse. For the most part, the United States can pursue its own macroeconomic policy with only scant regard for what is being done in the other two countries, whereas they cannot ignore U.S. policy.

This asymmetry existed before NAFTA came into existence. NAFTA, however, may permit greater consultation on these issues than existed before. In this sense, NAFTA expands the sovereign reach of the two weaker countries.

The $20 billion financial rescue package to Mexico by the United States was an indication of the U.S. inability to completely stand aside when its near neighbor is in trouble. This is not a NAFTA phenomenon, although the magnitude of the loan may have been influenced by the existence of NAFTA. The United States mounted rescue packages in pre-NAFTA days, in 1976 and again in 1982, but the amounts were much more modest. There were successive reschedulings of Mexico's external debt during the 1980s.

The primary objective of U.S. policy toward Mexico has always been to assure maximum social stability. Instability has repercussions such as augmented undocumented immigration in the United States. The United States in the past has given higher priority to stability than to democracy in Mexico. Today, the reasoning is that greater democracy reinforces stability. Greater prosperity also reinforces stability, hence NAFTA. It has become evident that faulty macroeconomic policy in Mexico can bring on instability, and it is now clear that Mexican policy will be subject to greater oversight than it was earlier. This is another example of asymmetrical dependence—of the fact that national control over policies is greater for powerful than for weaker nations.

Yet, one should not push too far the sacrifice of sovereignty inherent in NAFTA. What NAFTA does is push one step further the tendency that has long existed for sacrificing some national prerogatives in exchange for compensating benefits. The basic aspects of sovereignty—on how a country is governed and the determination of key national policies—still remain largely in national hands.

Notes

1. Sen. George Wilson Malone, *Congressional Record*, March 31, 1949, vol. 95, p. 3556.

2. Ralph Nader, "Introduction: Free Trade and the Decline of Democracy," in *The Case Against Free Trade: GATT, NAFTA, and the Globalization of Corporate Power* (San Francisco: Earth Island Press and Berkeley: North Atlantic Books, 1993), 27.

3. One reason for approval undoubtedly was that the WTO was part of the broader enabling bill to put into effect the results of the Uruguay Round of trade negotiations in the General Agreement on Tariffs and Trade, and this legislation was handled under fast-track procedures that called for an up or down vote on the entire package. Is there a lesson here? Treat trade schizophrenia in big packages, not smaller, discrete parcels.

4. Nader, "Introduction: Free Trade and the Decline of Democracy," 2.

5. Pat Buchanan, "Back door bailout after the rout?" *Washington Times*, February 1, 1995.

6. This may be because the debate in the United States on NAFTA ratification was more open, more democratic, than in Mexico. But public opinion polls in Mexico during the ratification process consistently indicated higher levels of support for NAFTA than did polls in the United States.

7. The 10 percent figure comes from national income and product accounts. See *Economic Report of the President* (Washington, D.C.: GPO, 1994), 292 and 293.

8. Between 1982 and 1992, average annual growth in U.S. FDI abroad was 8.9 percent; average annual growth in U.S. exports was 7.5 percent. These percentages understate the growth in FDI because they are calculated on the basis of historical cost, not market value. They also overstate the growth of exports, which are calculated on current values and not adjusted for inflation. See Sidney Weintraub, *NAFTA: What Comes Next?* (Westport, Conn.: Praeger for the Center for Strategic and International Studies, 1994), 19.

9. The prevailing U.S. sentiment seems to run as follows, with apologies to Shakespeare: "A borrower be, but not a lender."

10. Conrad Weiler, "GATT, NAFTA and State and Local Powers," *Intergovernmental Perspective* 20, no. 1 (Fall 1993-Winter 1994): 41.

11. These issues are discussed in Dan Morales, "The Evolving Protection of State Laws and the Environment: NAFTA from a Texas Perspective" (Occasional Paper No. 5, U.S.-Mexican Policy Studies Program, Lyndon B. Johnson School of Public Affairs, University of Texas at Austin, June 1994).

12. Michael Hart, *What's Next: Canada, the Global Economy and the New Trade Policy* (Ottawa: Centre for Trade Policy and Law, 1994), 20, states that 40 percent of Canadian trade is intrafirm and another 30 percent is the result of licensing and other intercorporate relations. Gail D. Fosler, *North American Outlook, 1995–1996* (New York: The Conference Board, 1995), 23, states that intrafirm shipments accounted for 63 percent of North American imports from Mexico in 1992.

13. Nader, "Introduction: Free Trade and the Decline of Democracy," 9.

14. Production-sharing with foreign countries of the type carried out in *maquiladora* plants is a worldwide phenomenon. Imports under U.S. provisions dealing with such products amounted to $56 billion in 1992, of which the U.S.-origin content was 27 percent. The Mexico-produced share of that total was $16.5 billion, of which the U.S.-origin content was 53 percent. That is, U.S. workers made more of the total value of imports from the Mexican *maquiladora* than they did of comparable coproduced imports from the rest of the world. U.S. International Trade Commission, *Production Sharing: U.S. Imports Under Harmonized Tariff Schedule Provisions 9802.00.60 and 9802.00.80, 1989–1992* (Washington, D.C.: USITC publication 2729, February 1994), 1–2, 4–6.

15. See, for example, Carlos Rico F., "Las relaciones mexicano-norteamericanos y los significados de la 'interdependencia,'" *Foro Internacional* 19 (October-December 1978). Rico later changed his view of U.S.-Mexican relations. But not all Mexicans did. For example, a prominent *panista*, a member of the conservative Partido Acción Nacional, José Angel Conchello, wrote in a widely sold book, *El TLC: Un callejón sin salida* (México, D.F.: Grijalbo, 1992) that NAFTA would "permit the North Americans to put their hand in all those internal matters as they see fit" and that Mexico would thereby lose an identity (286–287).

16. It differs from neoliberalism as used in international relations literature. Robert O. Keohane, "Neoliberal Institutionalism: A Perspective on World Politics," in *International Institutions and State Power*, ed. Robert O. Keohane (Boulder, Colo.: Westview Press, 1989), is a discussion of neoliberal institutionalism as a form of cooperation in a decentralized international system.

17. It is one of those interesting facts of hemispheric economic history that the most important advocate of the earlier version was the Economic Commission for Latin America under its then influential director, Raúl Prebisch; and the most articulate supporter of the current version is the same institution under the leadership of Gert Rosenthal. See *Open Regionalism in*

Latin America and the Caribbean (Santiago, Chile: United Nations Commission for Latin America and the Caribbean, 1994).

18. As with the term *neoliberalism*, here too there is a political science literature on the nature of cooperation among nations and achieving a balanced distribution of gains, however the word balanced is defined. See Helen Milner, "International Theories of Cooperation Among Nations: Strengths and Weaknesses," *World Politics* 44, no. 3 (April 1992): 466–496.

19. This theme is the subject of a leader in the *Economist*, "Hazardous Morals," February 11, 1995, 19–20.

20. The quoted language comes from a letter from Mickey Kantor, the U.S. Trade Representative, to Congressman Bill Archer, then the ranking Republican on the House Committee on Ways and Means, as reported in *Inside U.S. Trade*, October 22, 1993. The USTR position is supported in an analysis by Jerry Taylor, *NAFTA's Green Accords: Sound and Fury Signifying Little* (Washington, D.C.: Cato Institute, November 17, 1993).

21. Perhaps the strongest statement on this issue came from the U.S. judge on the three-member extraordinary challenge committee when writing on a softwood lumber case under chapter 19 of CUFTA. In his dissent against the majority decision of August 3, 1994, he questioned the constitutionality of removing the right of appeal from established U.S. courts.

22. See U.S. General Accounting Office, *Mexico's Financial Crisis* (Washington, D.C.: GAO, February 1996).

23. These conditions deal with shifting a budget deficit to surplus, limiting the growth of credit, drastically raising interest rates, and hypothecating the revenue from oil exports for loan repayment in the event of default. Each of these has been attacked by the political opposition in Mexico, from the left and from the right.

24. Indeed, my view is that many U.S. representatives and senators who wished to impose political as well as economic conditions on the loan package had in mind precisely the destruction of NAFTA. It was evident that Mexico could not accept insistence that it privatize Pemex, the national oil monopoly, or prevent its citizens from leaving the country to enter the United States, or cut off all economic relations with Cuba—yet all these conditions were proposed. What motive could there have been to propose unacceptable and unrelated conditions other than to provoke a confrontation?

25. This point was highlighted in a speech by Lawrence Summers, then under secretary of the treasury for monetary affairs, in Washington, D.C., on March 3, 1995.

26. Environmental opponents of the agreement were not mollified by the language in article 904:2 that permitted each party to establish the levels of protection it deemed appropriate in protecting its environment, health, and consumers.